Computing
Made Simple

Access 2000
STEPHEN
0750641827   1999

Access 2000 Business Edition
STEPHEN
075064611X   1999

Access 97 for Windows
STEPHEN
0750638001   1997

CompuServe 2000   NEW!
BRINDLEY
0750645245   2000

**Designing Internet Home Pages
2nd edition**
HOBBS
0750644761   1999

ECDL/ICDL Version 3.0   NEW!
BCD
0750651873   2000

Excel 2000
MORRIS
0750641800   2000

Excel 2000 Business Edition
MORRIS
0750646098   2000

Excel 97 for Windows
MORRIS
0750638028   1997

Excel for Windows 95 (V. 7)
MORRIS
0750628162   1996

Explorer 5
MCBRIDE, P K
0750646276   1999

Frontpage 2000
MCBRIDE, Nat
0750645989   1999

FrontPage 97
MCBRIDE, Nat
0750639415   1998

Mac and iBook   NEW!
BRINDLEY
075064608X   2000

**Internet In Colour
2nd edition**
MCBRIDE, P K
0750645768   1999

Internet for Windows 98
MCBRIDE, P K
0750645636   1999

MS DOS
SINCLAIR
0750620692   1994

Office 2000
MCBRIDE, P K
0750641797   1999

Office 97
MCBRIDE, P K
0750637986   1997

Outlook 2000   NEW!
MCBRIDE, P K
0750644141   2000

Photoshop
WYNNE-POWELL
075064334X   1999

Pocket PC   NEW!
PEACOCK
0750649003   2000

Powerpoint 2000
STEPHEN
0750641770   1999

Powerpoint 97 for Windows
STEPHEN
0750637994   1997

Publisher 2000
STEPHEN
0750645970   1999

Publisher 97
STEPHEN
0750639431   1998

Sage Accounts
McBRIDE
0750644133   1999

Searching the Internet
MCBRIDE, P K
0750637943   1998

Windows 98
MCBRIDE, P K
0750640391   1998

Windows 95
MCBRIDE, P K
0750623063   1995

Windows
PEACOCK
07506433

Windows
MCBRIDE
0750652

Windows NT
HOBBS
0750635118   1997

Word 2000
BRINDLEY
0750641819   1999

Word 2000 Business Edition
BRINDLEY
0750646101   2000

Word 97 for Windows
BRINDLEY
075063801X   1997

Word 7 for Windows 95
BRINDLEY
0750628154   1996

Works 2000
MCBRIDE, P K
0750649852   2000

UPCOMING in 2001

Basic Computer Skills
SHERMAN
075064897X

**ECDL/ICDL 3.0
Office 2000 Edition**
BCD
0750653388

Microsoft Project 2000
MURPHY
0750651903

ALL
YOU NEED
TO GET
STARTED!

MADE SIMPLE
BOOKS

Programming
Made Simple

C Programming
SEXTON
0750632445   1997

C++ Programming
SEXTON
0750632437   1997

COBOL
SEXTON
0750638346   1998

Delphi Version 5   NEW!
MORRIS
0750651881   2000

Delphi
MORRIS
0750632461   1997

HTML 4.0
MCBRIDE
0750641789   1999

Java
MCBRIDE, P K
0750632410   1997

Javascript
MCBRIDE, P K
0750637978   1997

Pascal
MCBRIDE, P K
0750632429   1997

Visual Basic
MORRIS
0750632453   1997

Visual C++
MORRIS
0750635703   1998

UPCOMING in 2001

Visual Basic Version 6
MORRIS
075065189X

ALL
YOU NEED
TO GET
STARTED!

MADE SIMPLE
BOOKS

Visual Basic 6
Made Simple

Stephen Morris

MADE SIMPLE
BOOKS

AMSTERDAM BOSTON HEIDELBERG LONDON NEW YORK OXFORD
PARIS SAN DIEGO SAN FRANCISCO SINGAPORE SYDNEY TOKYO

Made Simple
An imprint of Elsevier
Linacre House, Jordan Hill, Oxford OX2 8DP
200 Wheeler Road, Burlington, MA 01803

First published 2001
Reprinted 2002, 2003

TRADEMARKS/REGISTERED TRADEMARKS
Computer hardware and software brand names mentioned in this book are
protected by their respective trademarks and are acknowledged

British Library Cataloguing in Publication Data
A catalogue record for this book is available from the British Library

ISBN 0 7506 5189 X

For information on all Made Simple publications
visit our website at www.madesimple.com

Typeset by Butford Technical Publishing, Wombourne, South Staffs
Archetype, Bash Casual, Cotswold and Gravity fonts from Advanced Graphics Ltd
Icons designed by Sarah Ward © 1994
Printed and bound in Malta by Gutenberg Press

Contents

Preface

Visual Basic provides an excellent introduction to Windows programming, particularly for beginners. The 'Integrated Development Environment' allows you to create fully-fledged Windows applications with the minimum of effort and time. Since an application's windows are 'drawn' on the screen, you can always see what the eventual application will look like, without having to guess. All of this is achieved without writing a line of code and, as a result, Visual Basic bypasses the long-winded trial-and-error approach to designing screen displays of the older programming languages.

Creating the user interface is only the start, of course, and there is still a great deal of work to be done to complete an application. However, the Visual Basic programming language is both powerful and easy to master, so even complex tasks can be finished surprisingly quickly.

The latest version of Visual Basic, 6.0, has been designed specifically for the 32-bit environments of Windows 95 onwards. You cannot create 16-bit programs for Windows 3.1; for that you need the earlier version, 4.0. Although this book is based on VB 6.0, there is very little difference between versions 4, 5 and 6 or their programming languages. Therefore, instructions and programs in this book can be applied equally to any of the versions of the product. Where there are significant variations between the versions, the differences are noted.

This new edition of the book has been revised to cover the changes made in VB 6.0. There is also an additional chapter introducing Visual Basic's facilities for communicating with external databases and accessing the Internet.

This book is aimed at those who are new to programming, or new to Visual Basic. No previous programming experience is necessary, though familiarity with the use of Windows is assumed.

Visual Basic is a substantial programming language and, in a book of this size, it is only possible to give a brief introduction. However, the information given here should be enough to start you on some interesting projects and to show what may be achieved with practice.

Acknowledgements

I would like to thank Microsoft Corporation for their assistance while this book was in preparation.

1 Overview

Starting Visual Basic

Visual Basic provides a sophisticated Windows programming environment that is easy to use yet capable of producing powerful programs. Since it is a 'Visual' system you can create the visible part of a self-contained Windows application in a very short time, without the need to write any program code at all. You can then add short procedures for performing specific tasks, using an extended form of the traditional BASIC programming language. This book shows you how to create fully-fledged Windows applications, quickly and effectively.

Visual Basic editions

The latest version of Visual Basic comes in three different editions:

- Learning Edition – creates fully-functional Windows applications using a set of standard tools

- Professional Edition – adds specialised tools, a report writer and Internet capability

- Enterprise Edition – includes tools for setting up client/server applications

This book concentrates on the Learning Edition features, which are common to all three editions.

Windows versions

Visual Basic 6.0 is supplied only as a 32-bit version and must therefore be run under Windows 95 or later versions. Applications created with Visual Basic 6.0 can be run only under these versions of Windows; you will not be able to run your applications under 16-bit Windows 3.1.

Take note

The Visual Basic CD contains a number of development tools plus an extensive help system that covers the whole of the Microsoft Visual Studio environment. You do not have to install everything.

Installation

Visual Basic is installed in a similar way to most other Windows applications. Load the CD and run the SETUP program as follows:

Take note

If your CD is not drive D, replace D in the command with the drive letter.

1 Click on the Windows Start button and then on the Run option.

2 Type **D:\SETUP** in the Run box and click on OK.

3 Follow the instructions as they appear on screen.

At the end of the set-up process, Visual Basic will add an option to the Programs menu, leading to the main Visual Basic program plus some subsidiary programs.

Tip

If you are short of hard disk space you do not have to install the whole application; choose Custom rather than Typical from the installation options and deselect those parts of the system you do not need (they can always be added to the installation later by re-running the Setup program. Full installation of the Enterprise edition requires about 200 Mb of disk space.

Visual Basic folder

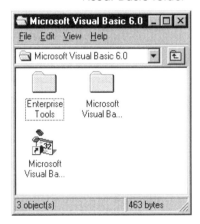

Tip

Create a Visual Basic folder and shortcut icon on the Windows desktop. In Explorer, open the Windows|Start Menu|Programs folder and copy the Microsoft Visual Basic 6.0 folder icon to the Windows|Desktop folder (click on the Visual Basic 6.0 folder, hold down [Ctrl] and drag the folder onto 'Desktop').

Running Visual Basic

The installation process will have created icons, which can be used to run the application.

Starting the program

1   Click on the Start button to display the Start menu.

2   Move the pointer to Programs and Microsoft Visual Basic 6.0.

3   Click on the Visual Basic 6.0 option.

Alternatively, if you have created a Visual Basic folder, double-click on the Visual Basic 6.0 icon.

Visual Basic folder

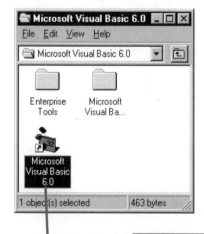

Double-click
here to run
Visual Basic

Take note

The operation of Visual Basic is the same in all versions of Windows. In this book, the illustrations are taken from the Enterprise edition running under Windows 95 but the same principles apply in other versions of Visual Basic and Windows.

4

The New Project window

As you enter Visual Basic 6.0, a New Project window is displayed. This dialog box effectively provides a menu for deciding what type of work you are going to do. To create your first application, double-click on **Standard EXE**. The main Visual Basic window is displayed.

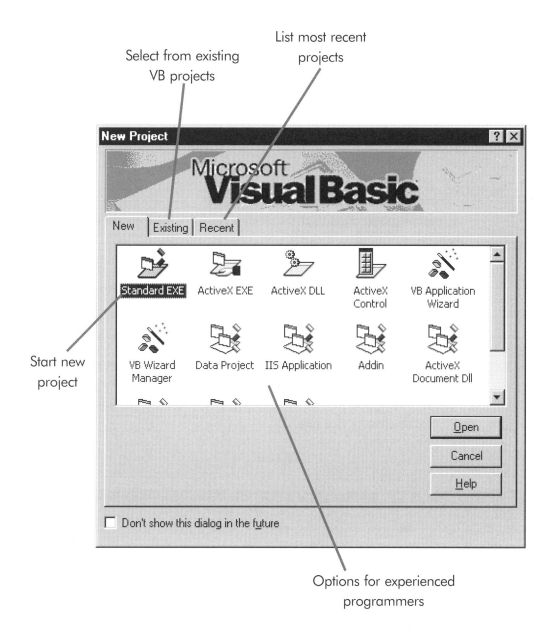

Visual Basic windows

The Visual Basic display is confusing when you first see it. The main Visual Basic window contains a number of other windows. Initially, six of these are open; others will pop up as you develop your application.

Take note

Four of the windows are 'docked' on the sides of the main window when you first come into Visual Basic. Any of them can be made to 'float' by dragging the title bar into the middle of the screen. They can then be resized.

Main window

The **main window** contains all the elements you would expect to find in a Windows application:

- The **title bar** contains the name of your current project (initially Project1) and the usual buttons for minimising, maximising and closing the window.

- The VB 6.0 **menu bar** includes 13 drop-down menus. Many of the options in these menus are described later in the book.

- The **toolbar** contains a number of icons that provide shortcuts to the most frequently used Visual Basic operations. On the right of the toolbar, two sets of figures provide size and position information about any selected Visual Basic element (see page 33).

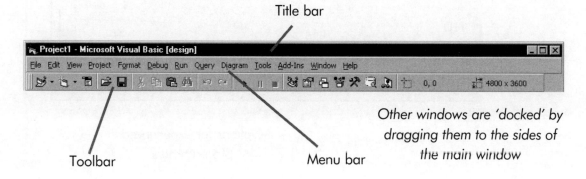

Title bar

Toolbar

Menu bar

Other windows are 'docked' by dragging them to the sides of the main window

Toolbox

Any window contains a number of different objects: command buttons, text boxes, labels and so on. These are called **controls**. When you are creating a window within Visual Basic, these controls can be added by dragging them from the **toolbox**. The pointer icon in the top left-hand corner of the toolbox is used for selecting existing controls so that they can be moved, resized or changed in some other way.

The toolbox controls are described in detail in Chapter 3.

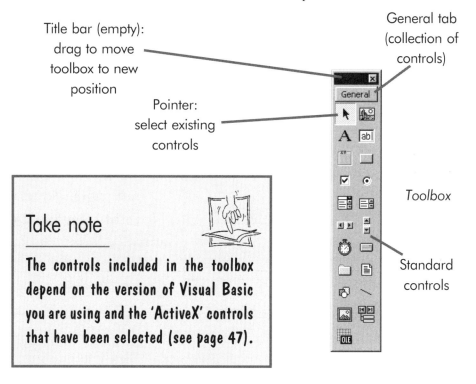

Title bar (empty): drag to move toolbox to new position

Pointer: select existing controls

General tab (collection of controls)

Toolbox

Standard controls

Take note

The controls included in the toolbox depend on the version of Visual Basic you are using and the 'ActiveX' controls that have been selected (see page 47).

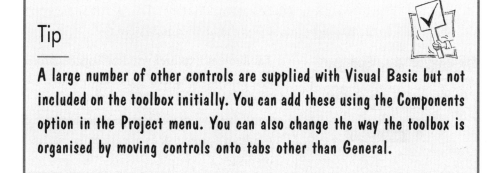

Tip

A large number of other controls are supplied with Visual Basic but not included on the toolbox initially. You can add these using the Components option in the Project menu. You can also change the way the toolbox is organised by moving controls onto tabs other than General.

Form1 and Form Designer window

A Visual Basic application usually consists of one or more windows. At the design stage, these windows are called **forms**. To start you off, Visual Basic supplies a single form, called Form1. This form will be renamed and resized when you begin to develop the application; other forms will be added as required. For Visual Basic 6.0, the forms are held in the Form Designer window.

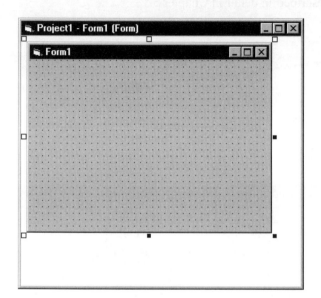

Take note

It is possible to create an application that has no forms at all: for example, an application to display a reminder at a specific time. In such cases, you need to delete Form1 – see page 24.

Project Explorer window

For each window in your final application there is a corresponding Visual Basic form, and each form has its own file on disk. Usually, there is also at least one file containing the program code for the application and, if your forms use any third-party tools, these will be held in additional files. All these files go together to make up the **project** from which the application is built.

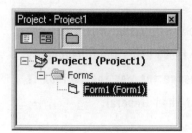

The Project Explorer window lists the project files. You can add existing files to a project or remove files. A file can be part of more than one project; for example, you may use the same window in two independent applications. Removing a file from a project does not affect the file itself; it is still intact on disk.

Properties window

Each form, and each control on a form, has a set of **properties**. These determine the appearance of the form or control and the way in which it behaves. A form has properties that specify how big it is and where it is on the screen, whether it is visible when the application starts, whether it has Minimise and Maximise buttons, and so on. Most controls have a large number of properties, some of which are similar to those of forms. For instance, a command button has the same size and position as a form but also includes properties to determine which keys can be used to activate it. Each type of control has a different set of properties. For each control, you can change the settings of individual properties (so all command buttons have the same properties but their settings are different).

The Properties window displays the properties for the selected form or control, and allows you to change their settings. Some of the more important properties are described in Chapters 2 and 3.

Form or control whose
properties are shown

Properties

Settings

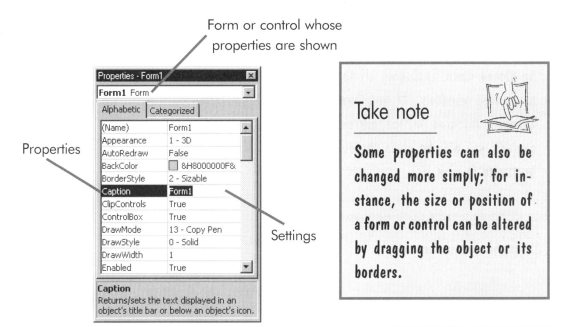

Take note

Some properties can also be changed more simply; for instance, the size or position of a form or control can be altered by dragging the object or its borders.

Form Layout window

The Form Layout window helps you determine the initial positions of the forms on the screen when the application is run. (Not available in VB 4.0.)

View options

Any of the Visual Basic windows can be cleared from the screen by clicking on the Close button in the top right-hand corner of the window.

To redisplay the toolbox, Project Explorer window, Properties window or Form Layout window, click on the appropriate option in the View menu; to redisplay Form1 and the Form Designer window, double-click on Form1 in the Project Explorer window (or click on Form1 and then on the View Object button).

The Visual Basic windows can also be moved by dragging their title bars or resized by dragging their corners or edges. The Maximise button on the Form Designer expands the window to fill the remaining space in the main window.

Take note

If you close the main window, the entire Visual Basic application will be closed down, including all the associated windows. If you have changed anything in the current project, you will be given the opportunity to save it.

Click here
to close

Click to
redisplay form

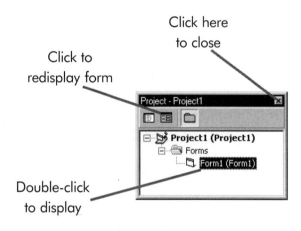

Double-click
to display

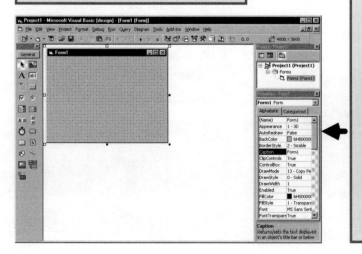

Tip

To make the screen as uncluttered as possible, maximise the main window and Form Designer, dock the toolbox, Project Explorer and Properties window, and close the Form Layout window.

Getting help

The printed documentation supplied with Visual Basic is very limited. However, Visual Basic holds all the information you will need in the form of on-line help. The VB 6.0 help is provided by the MSDN Library. The library is in the same format as a web browser, with the addition of a contents pane on the left-hand side. Because the help is very extensive you will probably not have installed all the files and you will be asked to load the MSDN CD when you select a help topic.

You can get on-line help in a number of ways:

● Click on Help in the menu bar at the top of the main window and then on Contents in the drop-down menu. This leads to the Help Contents window, where a number of 'books' are displayed. Double-clicking on the books and the topics they contain eventually takes you to a help screen.

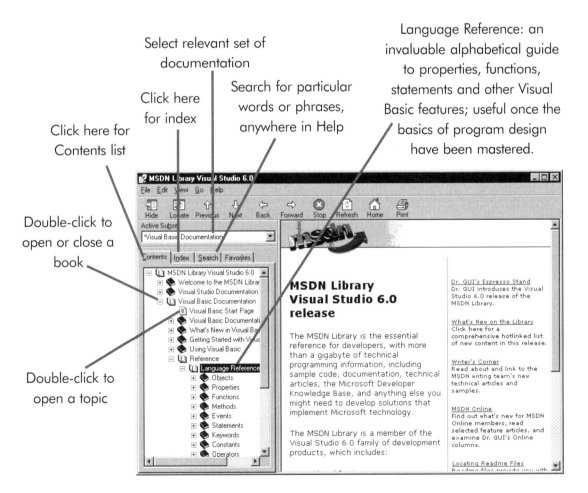

Select relevant set of documentation

Language Reference: an invaluable alphabetical guide to properties, functions, statements and other Visual Basic features; useful once the basics of program design have been mastered.

Click here for index

Search for particular words or phrases, anywhere in Help

Click here for Contents list

Double-click to open or close a book

Double-click to open a topic

- Select Help|Index or click on the Index tab in the Help window to display the Index list. The main part of this window lists the topics available in on-line help; you can either scroll through the list or start typing in the text box at the top to go straight to an item in the index. Double-click on an index item; this will either show the corresponding help or list relevant topics.

- After viewing a topic, click on the Help Topics button to go back to the Help Contents or Index.

- Press function key **[F1]** (context-sensitive help) to go straight to the topic relating to your current activity. For instance, if you click on a window and press **[F1]** you will get information on that window; if you click on a toolbox icon and press **[F1]**, details of the control and how to use it will be displayed.

You can also get context-sensitive help on specific parts of a form, object properties, error messages and individual keywords when writing code.

When you have finished with the help screen, remove it by clicking on the Close button.

Type text to find index entry

Double-click on an item to show related topics

Double-click on a topic to display help screen

Leaving Visual Basic

You can get out of Visual Basic at any time, either temporarily (while you work on some other application) or permanently.

Suspending Visual Basic

To suspend Visual Basic temporarily, click on the Minimise button on the main window and then start another application.

To get back into Visual Basic, use one of these methods:

● If Visual Basic was minimised, click on the VB project taskbar button.

● If any part of the Visual Basic window is visible, click on it.

● Press **[Alt-Esc]** or **[Alt-Tab]** repeatedly to cycle through the open applications until Visual Basic is active.

The program will be exactly as you left it.

Exiting Visual Basic

To close down Visual Basic altogether, select File|Exit. Alternatively, click on the Close button on the main window. If you have made any changes to the current project you are asked if you want to save them:

● Click on Yes (or press **[Enter]**) to save the changes. (If this is the first time the project has been saved, a filename will be needed – see page 25.)

● Click on No to abandon the changes – no further confirmation is requested.

● Click on Cancel (or press **[Esc]**) to continue working in Visual Basic.

If you attempt to close down the computer without ending Visual Basic, Windows will close Visual Basic for you and the same options will be given for any unsaved projects.

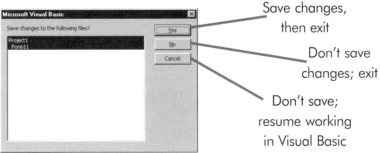

Save changes, then exit

Don't save changes; exit

Don't save; resume working in Visual Basic

Exercises

1   Start Visual Basic and identify the windows that are displayed.

2   Close individual windows and then re-open them again. Move the windows to more convenient positions; resize them where appropriate. Maximise the main window and Form Designer window.

3   Search for help relating to the Project Explorer window.

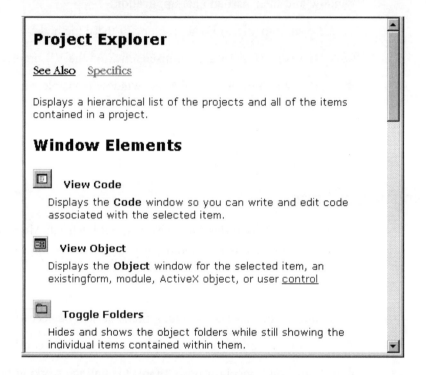

4   Minimise the main Visual Basic application and then re-activate it.

5   Exit Visual Basic.

For help with these exercises, see page 174.

2 Forms

The first form

Any Windows application is made up of one or more distinct **windows**. A window can be used to display information, to allow the user to enter data or to provide options for the user to select. At the development stage, the windows that make up a finished Visual Basic application are called **forms**. The forms you create become the windows through which the user accesses your application.

It is up to you, when designing a form, to decide how the window will behave: whether it is on-screen initially; whether the user can minimise or resize it; and so on. However, you should remember that once a window has been displayed it is the user who decides the order in which things happen and when the window will be closed down. The more objects (buttons, scroll bars, text boxes etc.) you put on a form, the less control you have over the user's actions.

A form starts off as an empty window, which may have a title bar and control buttons (Control-menu box, Minimise button, Maximise button, Close button). Within it, you may add other objects: buttons, lists, check boxes etc.

Form files

The details of each form are stored in a separate **form file**, with an FRM extension. This holds information such as the initial size of the form, its position and so on.

There will usually be some Visual Basic code attached to the form, determining how the application will respond when the user takes action on the window's

Take note

Forms are also used for most dialog boxes (e.g. those to select a file or enter a password) though some simple message boxes can be created as and when required within the code (see page 93).

Tip

Because a form is totally self-contained (the form file contains both a description of the form and all the code attached to it), the same form can be re-used in other applications. This means that all your applications can have the same 'look and feel', as well as reducing the amount of time you spend creating applications.

controls. For instance, when the user closes the window, the code attached to the form should take any necessary action on data that has been entered and then remove the window. The code for a particular form is stored in the form file.

The forms in an application are listed in the Project Explorer window: in each case, the name of the form file is given alongside the form name, in brackets.

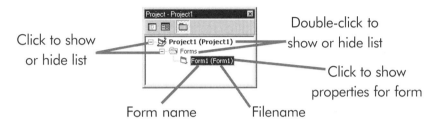

Click to show or hide list

Double-click to show or hide list

Click to show properties for form

Form name

Filename

Form1

Visual Basic supplies a default form to start the project: Form1. You can use this as your application's front-end window. The form can be customised as follows:

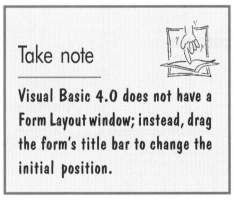

Take note

Visual Basic 4.0 does not have a Form Layout window; instead, drag the form's title bar to change the initial position.

1   Increase or decrease the size of the window by dragging one of the form's corners or its borders.

2   Move the form to a suitable position by dragging the Form1 box inside the Form Layout window; this will be the window's initial position when the program is run.

Other changes to the window and the way in which it behaves are made by altering the form's properties.

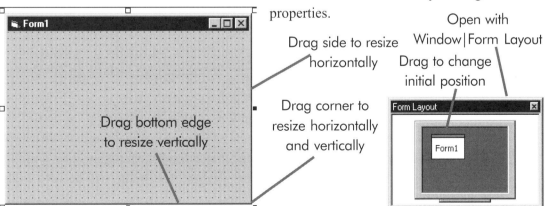

Drag side to resize horizontally

Open with Window|Form Layout

Drag to change initial position

Drag corner to resize horizontally and vertically

Drag bottom edge to resize vertically

Form properties

The appearance and behaviour of a window are determined by the corresponding form's **properties**. These specify such details as the size and position of the window, whether it can be minimised or closed, and so on. For each property, there is a single **setting**.

When you click on Form1 in the Project Explorer window, the properties are listed in the Properties window, in the left-hand column. The corresponding settings are shown on the right. Any property can be changed by clicking on the appropriate line. In some cases, there are a fixed number of options and you must choose from a drop-down list; for others, a value for the setting can be typed in directly.

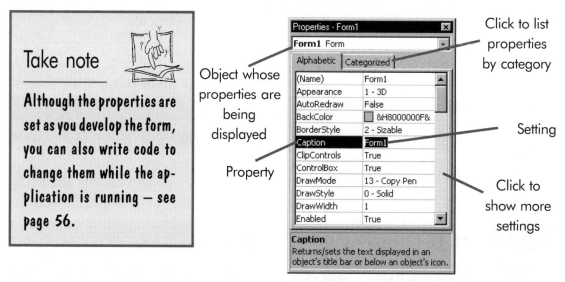

Take note

Although the properties are set as you develop the form, you can also write code to change them while the application is running – see page 56.

Object whose properties are being displayed

Property

Click to list properties by category

Setting

Click to show more settings

Name and Caption

The **Name** of the form is the name that appears in the Project Explorer window; the **Caption** is the piece of text that appears in the title bar (for the front-end window, usually the application title). Either can be changed by clicking on the existing setting and typing over it.

The Name property is shown in brackets so that it appears at the top of the alphabetic property list. Its setting should be changed to something that will tell you what the form does. By convention, the first three characters should be 'frm': for example, 'frmFront' for the front-end window. The Name will be used in the creation of the filename.

The border style

The **BorderStyle** property specifies the type of border and the elements that may appear in the title area. The most useful options are:

0 - None
There is no border; the window has no title bar or control buttons – useful for message boxes.

1 - Fixed Single
The window may have a title bar, Control-menu box, Close button, Minimise button and Maximise button. The user cannot change the window size by dragging the border. This style is used for windows with a fixed number of controls (e.g. data-entry forms).

2 - Sizable
The window may have any of the Fixed Single controls and may also be resized by the user. This is the default for all new forms and is used anywhere that the user may need to resize the form (e.g. text windows, spreadsheets, pictures).

3 - Fixed Dialog
The window is a dialog box. It may have a title bar and Control-menu button but cannot have the other control buttons. It cannot be resized by the user.

Two other options, 4 and 5, are used in the creation of toolbars. For more information on these options, see the on-line help.

To select a border option, click on BorderStyle. A down-arrow button appears on the right. Click on this, and a drop-down list is displayed. Click on one of the options in the list to change the setting.

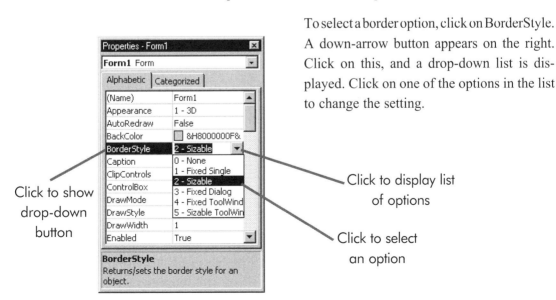

Click to show drop-down button

Click to display list of options

Click to select an option

Title bar and buttons

If BorderStyle is 0, the window will have no title bar and therefore no buttons. For any other setting a title bar is displayed and may contain the usual Windows buttons. The inclusion of a Control-menu box, Minimise button and Maximise button are determined by the settings of the **ControlBox**, **MinButton** and **MaxButton** properties respectively.

Each of these properties has two possible settings: True or False. The True setting indicates that the button is included (and therefore that the user may click on it); False means that the button will not be available.

The Close button is included only when there is a Control-menu box.

Position and size

The size of a form can be altered by dragging its borders; its position can be modified in the Form Layout window. When you do so, you change the following properties:

Left	Distance of left border from left-hand edge of screen
Top	Distance of top border from top of screen
Width	Width of form (including borders)
Height	Height of form (including borders and title bar)

For precise form size and position, these settings can be entered directly in the Properties window (where they can be found in the **Position** category). Entering the settings also ensures consistency between windows.

All sizes are measured in twips. There are 20 twips to a point (the units used for measuring font size). Since there are 72 points to an inch, there are 1440 twips to the inch (about 567 per centimetre). These sizes relate to the form when printed, not as displayed on screen. For high-resolution screens, text appears much smaller and more can be fitted on the screen; in a similar way, windows will appear smaller and take up less space on the screen.

Tip

When developing on a high-resolution screen, remember that end users may have screens of lower resolution. Either make sure that windows will have an initial position towards the left and top of the screen, or get the user's screen dimensions and use them to calculate the position and size at run time — see Chapter 4.

Take note

The values of Left, Top, Width and Height are shown in the two co-ordinate boxes on the right of the toolbar.

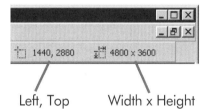

Left, Top   Width x Height

Visible and Enabled

A window should be displayed only when it is needed; this is controlled by the form's **Visible** property. When Visible is True, the window appears on the screen in its predefined position; when Visible is False, the window is hidden. Usually, the front-end form is visible and all other forms are initially hidden.

Only one window can be **active** at a time; the colour of the title bar is used by Windows to show which window is active. Clicking on a window makes it active (and deactivates all other windows). Even though a form is visible, you may not want the user to be able to access it. For instance, when a dialog box is displayed, you may not want the user to click on the window behind it until the dialog is closed. When the **Enabled** property for a form is True, users can click on the window to make it active; when the property is False, clicking on the window has no effect.

Saving the form

Like all other computer applications, you should save your work regularly. It can take a long time to set up a form just as you want it and it takes only a few seconds to save it.

As described above, the details of the form will be saved in a form file. This file holds everything that is needed to construct the form: its properties, its controls and their properties, and the code attached to the form.

You should create a new directory for the application's file. To save the current form, select File|Save *formname* As from the Visual Basic menu bar, change to the new directory, and give the file a suitable name. Visual Basic will suggest a filename, based on the first eight characters of the Name property (e.g. frmFront.frm for a form named frmFront). If you type a new name, Visual Basic will add an FRM extension. Remember that you are choosing a name for the form, not for the project as a whole.

After saving the file, the filename you specified appears in the Project Explorer window, to the right of the Name.

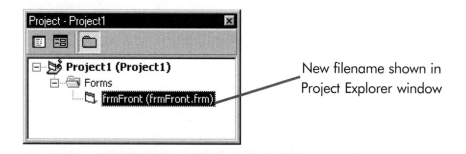

New filename shown in Project Explorer window

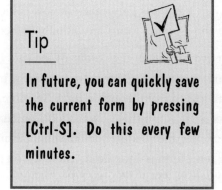

Tip

In future, you can quickly save the current form by pressing [Ctrl-S]. Do this every few minutes.

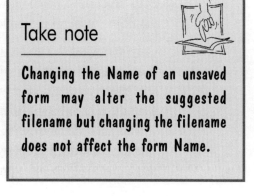

Take note

Changing the Name of an unsaved form may alter the suggested filename but changing the filename does not affect the form Name.

Adding new forms

Most applications need a number of Windows, and the forms for these can be created in much the same way as the first form. To add a new form, select Project|Add Form from the Visual Basic menu, click on the Form icon and then on Open. A blank form is displayed, with the same default settings as the original Form1. An entry for this form will be added to the Project Explorer window. The property settings can be changed by clicking on the form name in the Project Explorer and then changing values in the Properties window.

The following table lists suitable property settings for three different types of form that might be used in an application:

Property	Data Entry Window	Text Entry Window	Message Box
Name	frmData	frmText	frmMess1
Caption	Data Entry	Text Entry	Error
Left	4050	1365	3150
Top	1155	3690	3210
Width	6750	6810	4860
Height	5595	4005	1620
BorderStyle	1 - Fixed Single	2 - Sizable	3 - Fixed Dialog
ControlBox	True	True	False
MinButton	True	True	False
MaxButton	False	True	False

Having set up the new forms, each one should be saved with File|Save *formname* As. This option saves the **current** form, so make sure you have clicked on the form you want to save. Keep all forms for the project in the same directory.

After making further changes to a form, the file can be saved with File|Save *formname* (or click on the form and press **[Ctrl-S]**).

Adding existing forms

Existing form files can be added to the project at any time. Select Project|Add Form, click on the Existing tab and then choose the form file from the file list. In this way, you can restore forms that were previously removed. You can also add in forms that were created for other projects.

Take note

For Visual Basic 4.0, new forms are created with Insert|Form and existing forms are added with File|Add File.

Removing forms

If a form is no longer needed, it can be removed from the project. On the Project Explorer window, click on the form name and then select Project|Remove*formname*.

Although the form is removed from the project, the form file itself is unaffected and can be restored later if required.

If you remove Form1, you will be asked to select a Startup form when you next run the program; the Startup form is the first form to be displayed.

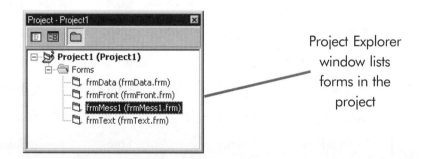

Project Explorer window lists forms in the project

Take note

Most messages boxes are created when needed within the code — see page 103.

Tip

Make sure you are changing the properties for the correct form. The name of the current form is shown at the top of the Properties window.

Saving and running

Usually, an application is made up of several windows, each of which is created from a form in a FRM file. The application as a whole has a **project file**, which defines the forms and other files that go together to make up the finished project. The project has only a single property, its Name; click on the project name at the top of the Project Explorer and then change the Name in the Properties window.

The current project can be saved with File|Save Project As. Again, save it in the project directory with a name that identifies the project as a whole. The file is given a VBP extension. If any form has changed, you will be prompted to save it first.

Suggested name – replace if necessary

New directory

Select directory

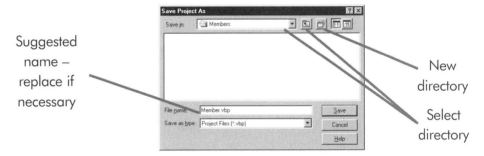

You will also be asked if you want to save the project in SourceSafe; this is a file management system, which stores previous versions of your files, so that you can recover them at any time. SourceSafe is particularly useful if several people are working on the project at the same time.

Running the application

To test the program, select Start from the Run menu (or press **[F5]**). (For earlier VB versions you must select a Startup form.) The first window should pop up straight away. It may not appear very impressive but all the buttons on the window should behave as you would expect. The Minimise and Maximise buttons (if included) reduce the application to an icon or blow it up to full-screen size, respectively. The window can be moved or resized (depending on the setting for BorderStyle). Other windows are not visible yet – you need to add some program code before they can be seen. Finally, you can close the application by clicking on the Close button in the top right-hand corner of the window.

You can switch back to Visual Basic while the application is running but you are limited in the changes you can make. If necessary, you can halt the application by selecting Run|End.

Exercises

The exercises in this book build up an application for storing membership details for an organisation. This application can be modified to suit many other purposes, such as a contacts database or a program to store records of correspondence.

1 Create a new directory.

2 Start a new project.

3 Create a front-end form, with a Minimise button but no Maximise button. The form should be of fixed size, with a suitable title. Name it 'frmMainMenu' and save it in a file called frmMainMenu.frm.

4 Create a form for entering data, again with no Maximise button and of fixed size. Name it 'frmDetails' and save it with a suitable filename.

5 Create a form for entering text. This form should be sizable. Name it 'frmComments' and save it with a suitable filename.

6 Change the Name of the project to 'Members'.

7 Save the project with the filename Members.vbp.

8 Run the application to check that the front-end window is displayed correctly. Save the changes.

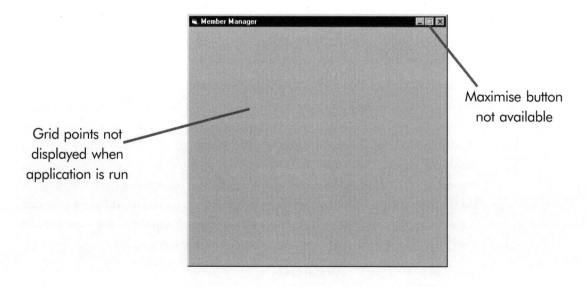

Maximise button not available

Grid points not displayed when application is run

For help with these exercises, see page 174.

3 Controls

Adding controls

All windows have one or more **controls**. These are objects that display information or allow the user to perform an action: for instance, command buttons, text boxes, option buttons and scroll bars.

Any combination of controls can be placed on a form but you should remember that when the application is run the user will be free to use the controls in any order (subject to any restrictions you impose at development time).

For example, the message box that is displayed if you remove the first form and then try to run an application contains, in effect, four controls: two buttons (marked OK and Help), a label (containing the text of the message) and an image control (containing the icon). The program forces you to click on one of the buttons but it's up to you which you choose. The action taken by the program depends on which button is clicked.

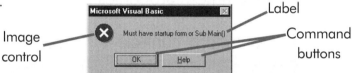

Image control — Label — Command buttons

The toolbox

Visual Basic supplies a number of standard controls for use on forms. These are represented by icons in the toolbox. Controls can be added to a form in two ways:

●   Click on the control in the toolbox, then drag the pointer over the area of the form to be covered by the control.

●   Double-click on the control to create an object of default size on the form.

In either case, you can change the size and position later (see *Control properties* below). The standard controls are described from page 38 onwards.

To remove a control from the form, click on it (so that square 'sizing handles' are shown on the corners and sides) and then press the **[Del]** key.

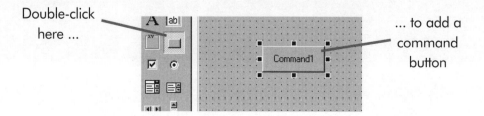

Double-click here ...   ... to add a command button

Control properties

The appearance and behaviour of a control is determined by its **properties**, in the same way as for a form. The properties include not only cosmetic items – the size, colour and position of the control, for example – but also those characteristics that affect the way a control is used: the text shown on it, the user actions that are allowed etc.

The properties are different for each type of control and in each case the system provides a default. Most defaults are quite satisfactory so there are usually only a very few properties that need to be changed.

As for forms, you will set the properties when developing the project but they may also be changed while the application is running.

Some properties apply to most or all of the controls – for instance, every control has a Name – and most can be revised. The most important properties are described below for the standard controls.

A number of other, more advanced properties are included in most controls and may be useful when an application reaches a later stage of development. You are unlikely to use these properties often but it is worth knowing they are there.

Changing properties

To change the properties for a control, first click on the control so that it is selected. Small square 'handles' will appear at each corner and in the middle of each side. The Properties window will show the name of the control at the top (initially a default name, consisting of the control type and a number); you will see the properties that are listed change each time you select a different type of control.

Remember that all controls of the same type will have the same properties but each control will be given different settings. Therefore, when you click on different controls of the same type you will see the same list of properties but with different settings in each case. For example, all command buttons have Name, Width and Caption properties; the settings for one button may be cmdOK, 1440 and OK respectively, and for another, cmdHelp, 720 and Help.

To change the control properties, click on a control and on a property in the Properties window. Then either type a new setting in the right-hand column or (where appropriate) select the setting from a drop-down list.

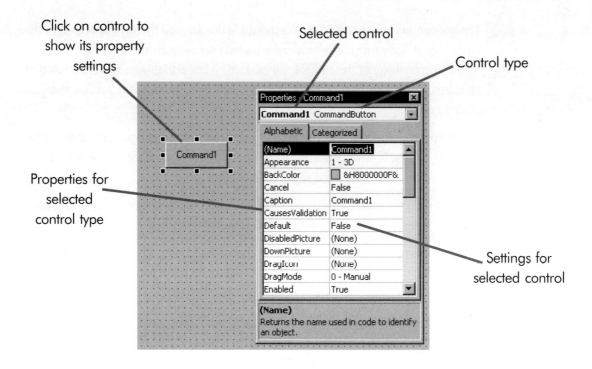

Click on control to show its property settings

Selected control

Control type

Properties for selected control type

Settings for selected control

Multiple properties

You can select a group of controls in one of the following ways:

- Hold down the **[Shift]** key and then click on two or more controls. Each time you click on an additional control, the other selected controls are identified with **white** sizing handles.

- Move the pointer to a blank area of the form and then drag it over the controls. Any control that is at least partly covered by the marked rectangle is given white or blue sizing handles.

- A control can be removed from the group by holding down **[Shift]** and clicking on it again.

This method is normally used for dragging controls to another part of the form but it can also be used for changing the settings for all the marked controls at the same time. If you change a setting in the Properties window, the setting is applied to all selected controls; for instance, you can change the width of a group of controls.

Common properties

A large number of properties are common to all or most controls; these provide the basic functionality of the controls. Each type of control has its own additional properties, which regulate those features that are peculiar to the control. For instance, most controls can have their size and position changed but only a text box has a PasswordChar property, which allows the box to be used for entering a password. The most useful properties are described here.

Name

Every control has a **Name**, which is used when referring to the control in a procedure (for instance, when changing the control's properties at run time). Visual Basic gives each new control a default name, consisting of the control type and a number: Command1, Command2, ..., Text1, Text2 etc.

You should change these to something more meaningful. Although you could keep the defaults, you should change the Name for all controls, even those you think you are unlikely to use in your program.

The rules for names are as follows:

● Names can be up to 40 characters long but for ease of use you should keep them much shorter than this.

● Names may consist of letters, numbers and underscore (_) characters; no other characters or spaces are allowed.

● Names must start with a letter. You can use numbers or underscores anywhere in the Name apart from the first character.

● Upper and lower case letters are treated as being the same but a mixture can be used to make the name easier to identify (cmdSaveAs is more recognisable than cmdsaveas but both refer to the same control).

By convention, the first three characters are lower-case letters indicating the type of control; all command buttons begin 'cmd', all text boxes 'txt' and so on. A list of naming conventions is given under *Standard controls* on page 38. If you adopt the standard naming convention, stick to it for all controls.

You should change the Name for all new controls, even those you think you are unlikely to use in a procedure. For instance, labels may originally be fixed but later on you may want to vary them when the program is running.

Caption

Most controls have a **Caption**. This holds the item of text that appears on the surface of the control. The restrictions on the control Name do not apply to the Caption; this is a purely cosmetic piece of text.

You can include an & in front of a character in the Name to denote that character as an **access key**. When there is an access key, the control can be 'clicked' by pressing **[Alt]** and the access character together. The access key character is underlined in the control's caption. If you need to include an & in the Caption itself, type '&&'; only one & will be displayed.

It is usual to select the first letter of the Caption as the access key, unless that letter has already been used by another control on the same form (in which case you can select any suitable character in the Caption).

If two controls have the same access key, pressing that combination will select each one of them in turn. However, this is confusing for users and should be avoided.

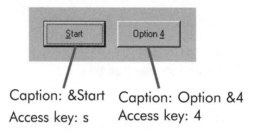

Caption: &Start
Access key: s

Caption: Option &4
Access key: 4

Text

Controls that allow users to type an entry have a **Text** property. In some cases, you can set a default value for the Text property, which is shown when the form is first displayed and which the user can then overwrite. For other controls, the Text property cannot be set during development but you can change it (and the user can add text) while the application is running.

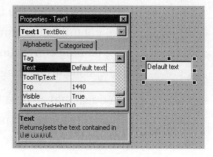

You can add read-only controls to the form (where the user cannot change the text) by changing the controls' Enabled property to False (see page 37).

Size and position

The size and position of a control are determined by the same set of four properties as for a form: **Width** and **Height** for the size, **Left** and **Top** for position. Left and Top give the position of the top-left corner of the control relative to the top-left corner of the inside of the form.

These properties can be changed either by dragging the sizing handles on the corners and sides of the control or by entering new settings directly. Usually, dragging the sizing handles is satisfactory, as it enables you to set the size and position by eye. For precise settings, however, the properties can be adjusted manually.

By default, the same units (twips) are used for controls as for forms. When you click on a control, the co-ordinate boxes in the toolbar show the current settings for these four properties.

Take note

For Visual Basic 4.0, use Tools|Options|Environment.

When developing a form there is a background grid of points for aligning controls. If you change the control size or position by dragging, the control corners 'snap' to the nearest grid points. The grid can be changed (or switched off) by choosing Tools|Options and clicking on the General tab; the Width and Height of the grid square can be changed and the grid snap can be turned off.

Click to turn off grid

Spacing of grid points (twips)

Click to stop controls snapping to grid

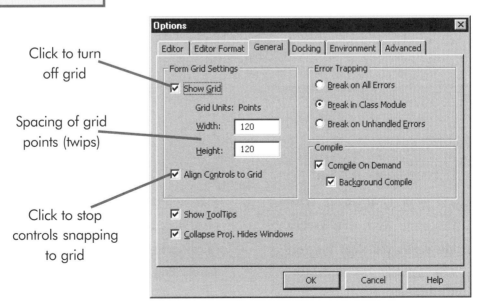

Fonts

If the control displays text, you can change the appearance with the **Font** property. When you click on the setting box, a small button (with three dots) appears on the right. Clicking on this displays the Font window, from which you can select the font, the style (bold, italic etc.) and the point size. You can also apply strikeout (a line through the middle of the text) and underline.

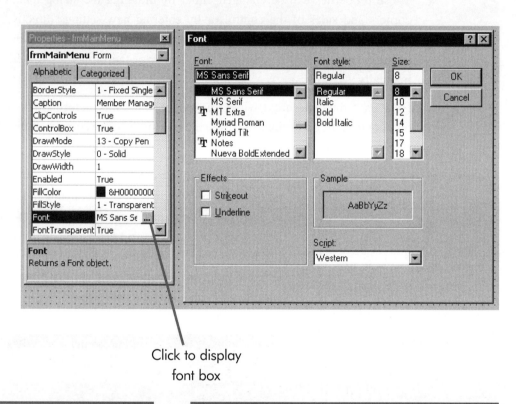

Click to display
font box

Tip

If you click on the Font list and move up and down using the arrow keys, the Sample box shows you what the text will look like.

Tip

Use only the standard Windows fonts, so that your application will always look the same, regardless of the machine running it. If you use third-party fonts, you must be prepared to supply these with your application.

Colour

The control's background colour is set by the **BackColor** property. For controls that display text or graphics, the colour of these is determined by **ForeColor**. The values for colours can be entered in one of two ways:

- Selecting from a palette
- Entering an RGB colour number

The easiest way to choose a colour is by clicking on the drop-down list in the setting box. You can select from a number of standard Windows colours (as set in the Control Panel) or from a colour palette. When you click on a colour square, a numeric code is entered in the setting box. The main disadvantage of these methods is that the range of colours is limited.

Alternatively, you can create your own colour by entering a numeric RGB code. Each colour on the screen is made up of three components – red, green and blue – in differing intensities. The colour is represented by a hexadecimal number in the form &H*bbggrr*&, where *rr* is the red component, *gg* green and *bb* blue. Each component can have a value between 00 (no colour) and hexadecimal FF (full intensity). The midpoint is 80.

Click to display
colour palette

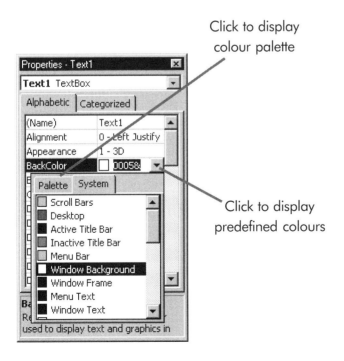

Click to display
predefined colours

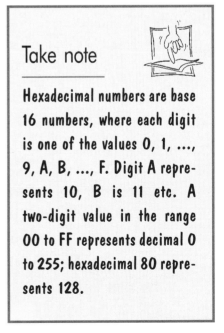

Take note

Hexadecimal numbers are base 16 numbers, where each digit is one of the values 0, 1, ..., 9, A, B, ..., F. Digit A represents 10, B is 11 etc. A two-digit value in the range 00 to FF represents decimal 0 to 255; hexadecimal 80 represents 128.

Tab stops and focus

When the user clicks on a window, the window is said to have the **focus**; that is, it is the active window. The title bar of the window with the focus has a different colour to the others. (In the default Windows colours, the window with the focus has a blue title bar, the rest are grey.) Only one window can have the focus at any one time.

Similarly, one (and only one) control on the window has the focus. This is usually indicated by a thicker border around the control, by highlighting or by the appearance of a cursor in text boxes.

When the user presses the **[Tab]** key, the focus moves from one control to the next. The order in which the focus moves is determined by two properties: **TabStop** and **TabIndex**. The TabStop setting specifies whether or not the control can have the focus (a setting of True if it can), while TabIndex gives the order in which the controls have the focus. Each control on the form has a unique tab index number. Initially, the tab index numbers match the order in which the controls were added to the form.

To change the tab order, change the TabIndex setting for a control. All the index numbers will be updated to take account of the new order. For example, if there are four controls on the form, the index numbers will be 0, 1, 2 and 3. To move the last control into second place, change its index number from 3 to 1. The system will then renumber the two controls in the middle from 1 and 2 to 2 and 3 respectively. By changing the tab index for several objects, you can put the controls into any order you like.

Take note

All controls have a TabIndex number but those for which TabStop is False are ignored. No two controls on a form have the same TabIndex.

Tip

Don't worry about the tab settings until the form is complete — then you can set the tab index for all the controls at once, when you have a better idea of the order you want.

Visible and Enabled

The **Visible** property determines whether the control can be seen and **Enabled** decides whether it can be used. As a general rule, it is less confusing for the user if controls are always visible but not necessarily enabled. When a control is not enabled (its Enabled setting is False), any text displayed on it is grey and clicking on the control has no effect. Naturally, if a control is not visible (its Visible setting is False), the user cannot click on it and its Enabled property is irrelevant.

For example, you may have a Save button on your form that is enabled only when new data has been entered in text boxes. (The alternative would be to make the Save button visible when a change is made to the data but a button suddenly popping up on the window is disconcerting for the user.)

The Enabled property can also be used for making a text box read-only. If you set Enabled to False the user can see the text but cannot change it.

The Visible property may be used where the value of one control affects the applicability of others. For instance, on an accounts form a pair of radio buttons may allow you to choose between a payment and a receipt. Other controls on the form – such as a text box for the cheque number – will be made visible depending on the radio button that is clicked. When the user clicks the payment button, the cheque number is made visible; when the receipt button is clicked, the Visible property for the cheque number box is set to False while a text box containing the delivery date could be made visible

In another case, a command button may be clicked to display additional information in the window. When the button is clicked, the Visible property on a text box is set to True.

Tip

Two controls may occupy the same space on the form, providing they are never both visible at the same time. For instance, the same area may be used for a cheque number for payments and the delivery date for receipts.

Standard controls

The Visual Basic toolbox contains the following standard controls:

Control	Name Prefix	Object Name	Default Property
Picture box (p154)	pic	PictureBox	Picture
Label (p40)	lbl	Label	Caption
Text box (p41)	txt	TextBox	Text
Frame (p44)	fra	Frame	Caption
Command button (p39)	cmd	CommandButton	Value
Check box (p43)	chk	CheckBox	Value
Option button (p43)	opt	OptionButton	Value
Combo box (p67)	cbo	ComboBox	Text
List box (p64)	lst	ListBox	Text
Horizontal scroll bar (p46)	hsb	HScrollBar	Value
Vertical scroll bar (p46)	vsb	VScrollBar	Value
Timer (p47)	tmr	Timer	Enabled
Drive list box (p138)	drv	DriveListBox	Drive
Directory list box (p138)	dir	DirListBox	Path
File list box (p138)	fil	FileListBox	FileName
Shape (p155)	shp	Shape	Shape
Line (p155)	lin	Line	Visible
Image (p154)	img	Image	Picture
Data control (p47)	dat	Data	Caption
OLE control (p47)	ole	OLE	–

The toolbox may show other controls, depending on the version that is being run and any controls that have been added. Visual Basic allows you to add other controls (called **ActiveX** controls) using Project|Components (or, for VB 4.0, Tools|Custom Controls).

By convention, all forms start with 'frm' and menus begin with 'mnu'.

In this table:

- The Name Prefix is the three-character abbreviation that should be used when naming controls.

- The Object Name is the name under which the control can be found in the Visual Basic on-line *Language Reference*, which gives a detailed description of the controls, their properties and their uses.

- The Default Property is the property to which a value is given in procedures when no other property is specified.

The table also gives the page numbers where the controls are described in this book.

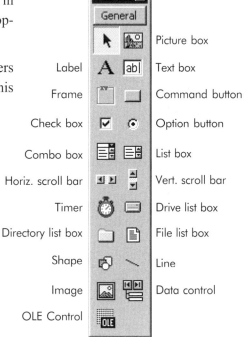

	Picture box
Label	Text box
Frame	Command button
Check box	Option button
Combo box	List box
Horiz. scroll bar	Vert. scroll bar
Timer	Drive list box
Directory list box	File list box
Shape	Line
Image	Data control
OLE Control	

Take note

The pointer icon in the top-left corner of the toolbox is not a control. Click on this icon when you want to select an existing control in order to make changes to the control's properties.

Command buttons

Command buttons are used for performing actions. A procedure is attached to each command button and is executed when the user clicks on the button. You cannot decide the order in which buttons are clicked but you do have full control over the action taken once the user has clicked a button.

The text that appears on the surface of the command button is held in the **Caption** property.

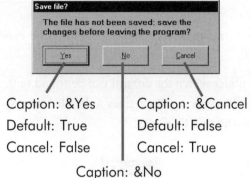

Caption: &Yes
Default: True
Cancel: False

Caption: &No
Default: False
Cancel: False

Caption: &Cancel
Default: False
Cancel: True

The **Default** property identifies the button that is activated when the user presses the **[Enter]** key; usually this is the OK button. Only one button on a form may have a Default setting of True; all others must be False.

In a similar way, only one button may have its **Cancel** property set to True; this is the button that is activated when the user presses **[Esc]** (usually the button with a Caption of 'Cancel').

The **Value** property (which can only be set at run time) indicates that the button has been clicked; setting the property to True effectively forces the button to be clicked.

Labels

The **label** control adds text to the form: titles, instructions, text for data-entry boxes and so on. The user cannot do anything with these controls but you may wish to change the text itself at run time; for example, after a file has been selected a label may be used to display the filename.

The text of the label is held in the **Caption**. The position of the text within the label area is set by the **Alignment** property: left-aligned, centred or right-aligned.

Alignment: 2 – Center
Font style: Bold
Font size: 14

Alignment: 1 – Right Justify
Font style: Regular
Font size: 8

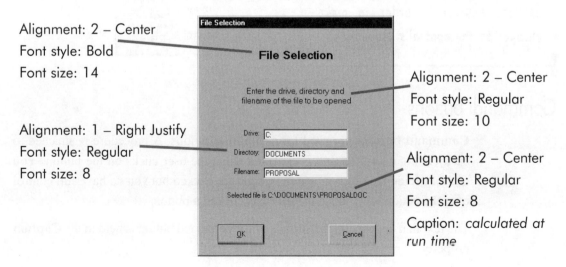

Alignment: 2 – Center
Font style: Regular
Font size: 10

Alignment: 2 – Center
Font style: Regular
Font size: 8
Caption: *calculated at run time*

If the text will not fit in the label area, setting **AutoSize** to True allows the label to expand its area if necessary. If you want the text of the label to spread over more than one line, set **WordWrap** to True; the label will expand downwards as the length of the text increases. Otherwise, if WordWrap is False, the label expands horizontally to fit the text.

To draw a box around the label, change the **BorderStyle** property to 1.

Text boxes

The **text box** provides the simplest method for the user to enter data. When the control has the focus, a vertical cursor is displayed and the user can make an entry.

The **Text** property contains the user's entry when it is complete; by setting this property during development you can supply a default value, which the user can either leave as it is or change.

By default, the **BorderStyle** property is 1, resulting in a box drawn around the edge of the text area. Change this to 0 to remove the box.

Text boxes do not have a Caption; since the text typed in the box can be changed by the user, it is held in the Text property instead. The lack of a Caption means that text boxes cannot be given an access key directly. However, you can get round the problem by placing a label control next to the text box; since a label control cannot be clicked, the access key on the label acts as an access key for the text box.

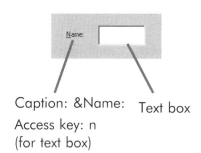

Caption: &Name: Text box
Access key: n
(for text box)

Take note

For a label control to contain the access key for a text box, the label must come immediately before the text box in the tab order – see page 36.

Setting **MultiLine** to True creates a text box with two or more lines of text. The **Alignment** setting places text on the left or right of the box, or centres it.

The **Locked** property, if set to True, stops the user from changing the text.

41

MaxLength sets a limit to the number of characters that can be entered in the box. For instance, a setting of 8 could be used when entering a password. If MaxLength is 0 (the default), the amount of text is limited only by the computer's memory.

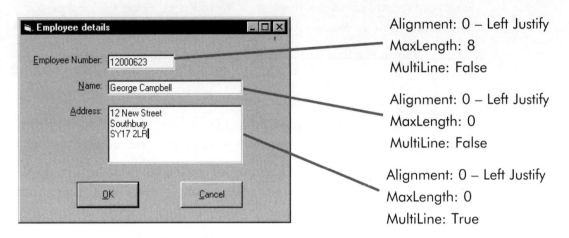

For large amounts of text, where MultiLine is True, you may want to add scroll bars. The **ScrollBars** property can take the following settings:

0   No scroll bars. Use this when the amount of text is limited.

1   Horizontal scroll bar. The user can keep typing to the right, beyond the end of the box. Use where there are no paragraphs (e.g. program code).

2   Vertical scroll bar. This is the most useful option, giving a clear indication of how much text has been typed and where the cursor is relative to the text as a whole.

3   Both scroll bars. Use this for text that can spread in both directions.

If there is no horizontal scroll bar, the text for a multi-line box automatically wraps to the next line when the right-hand edge of the box is reached. However, when there is no vertical scroll bar, the text will still scroll upwards when the box is full, unless you set MaxLength. Therefore, you should usually have a vertical scroll bar for multi-line text.

The **PasswordChar** property is useful when asking the user to enter a password. The setting can be any single character (though it is usually *); this character will be displayed regardless of what the user types but the actual entry will be held in the Text property.

42

Option buttons and check boxes

Option buttons and check boxes provide two different methods of giving the user choices.

 **Option buttons** usually appear in groups of two or more, and all the buttons on a form are interrelated (unless they are in a frame – see page 44). The control consists of a circle with a piece of text next to it. The text is held in the **Caption** property.

The **Alignment** property can be 0 or 1, depending on whether the text is to be to the right or left of the circle. The **Value** property has a setting of either True or False, depending on whether or not the button has been selected. Only one button can be selected at a time, so when the user clicks on an option button the Value for that button is set to True and for all other buttons to False.

Tip

You can have more than one group of option buttons on a window if you enclose them in frames – see below.

Check boxes work in a similar way, the main difference being that they operate independently of each other. As a result, the user may select several boxes at the same time by clicking on them – or turn all boxes off. The properties are similar except for **Value**, for which the possible settings are 0 (not selected), 1 (selected) and 2 (not available). For a setting of 2, the box and tick are greyed out and the Enabled property should be set to False.

Tip

The Value of 2 is useful when options are mandatory. For instance, the choice of an option button may make a particular check item essential.

To make a check box temporarily unavailable, set its Enabled property to False. It is less disconcerting for a user to see a check box greyed out that for it to disappear completely (by setting Visible to False).

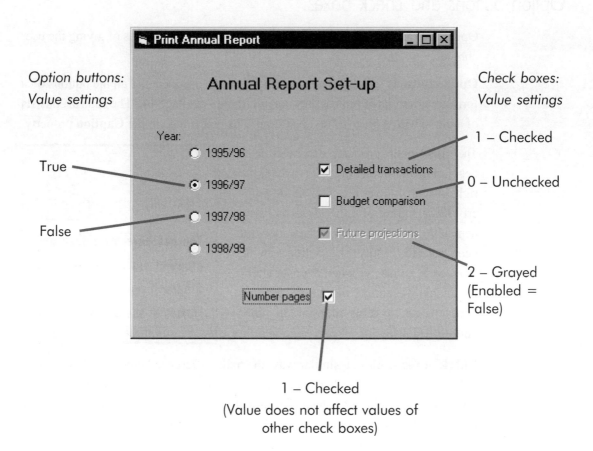

Option buttons:
Value settings

Annual Report Set-up

Check boxes:
Value settings

1 – Checked

Year:

○ 1995/96

True

◉ 1996/97

☑ Detailed transactions

0 – Unchecked

☐ Budget comparison

○ 1997/98

☑ Future projections

False

○ 1998/99

2 – Grayed
(Enabled =
False)

Number pages ☑

1 – Checked
(Value does not affect values of
other check boxes)

Frames

Frames allow you to group controls together. From a functional point of view, frames are needed if you want more than one set of option buttons on a screen. Option buttons inside a frame act as a group, independently of any other buttons. For this to work, you must add the frame to the form first and then insert the option buttons within the borders of the frame.

Frames can also be used to improve the appearance of the window. Apart from option buttons, any other group of controls can be placed within a frame, though this has no effect on the way they function.

The frame **Caption** is the piece of text overlaid on the top left-hand corner of the frame.

Select exactly one button from this group

Select any number of boxes from this group

Greyed boxes cannot be selected (Enabled = False)

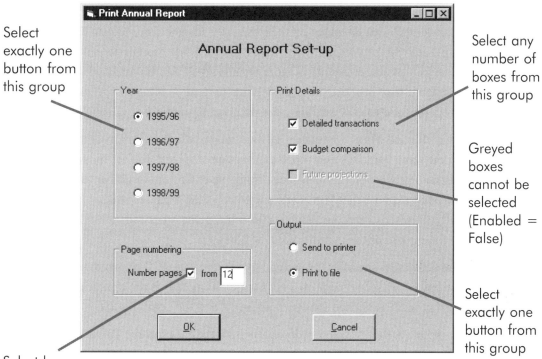

Print Annual Report

Annual Report Set-up

Year
- ○ 1995/96
- ○ 1996/97
- ○ 1997/98
- ○ 1998/99

Print Details
- ☑ Detailed transactions
- ☑ Budget comparison
- ☐ Future projections

Page numbering
Number pages ☑ from 12

Output
- ○ Send to printer
- ○ Print to file

OK   Cancel

Select exactly one button from this group

Select box independently of others on form

Scroll bars

Scroll bars frequently appear on text boxes but you can also add them in other places. They can be added on their own (for instance, to indicate the progress of some activity or as an alternative data entry method), though standalone scroll bars tend to look rather peculiar. More usually, they can be attached to the edge of windows (for instance, one displaying part of a bitmap). In such cases, the properties are usually set while the program is running.

The **Min** and **Max** properties give the limits of the values that can be represented by the scroll bar; the **Value** represents the current position of the button on the scroll bar, as a proportion of the distance from one end of the scroll bar to the other. For instance, suppose that Min is 100 and Max is 200. When the button is at the top (or left) of the scroll bar, the Value is 100; when at the other end, the Value is 200; and in the middle of the bar, the Value is 150.

SmallChange specifies the amount by which Value will change when an arrow at the end of the scroll bar is clicked; **LargeChange** gives the change in Value when the bar itself is clicked (between an arrow and the scroll button).

In the illustration, two procedures are used: the first sets the Text value of the text box to the scroll bar Value when the scroll bar is adjusted; the second revises the scroll bar Value (and hence the position of the button on the scroll bar) when the Text in the text box is changed. Information on procedures is given in Chapter 4.

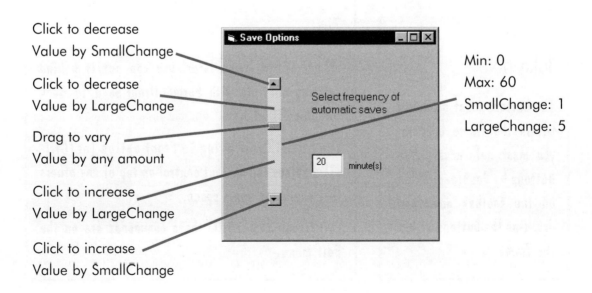

Click to decrease
Value by SmallChange

Click to decrease
Value by LargeChange

Drag to vary
Value by any amount

Click to increase
Value by LargeChange

Click to increase
Value by SmallChange

Min: 0
Max: 60
SmallChange: 1
LargeChange: 5

Other controls

In addition to the simple controls described above, there are a number of other standard controls on the toolbox:

- The **picture box** and **image** controls allow you to add bitmaps; picture boxes also provide simple drawing facilities, as do **shape** and **line** controls (see page 154).

- The **timer** lets you generate events at predefined times. (Add the control to the form and then set the Interval between timer events, giving a value in milliseconds.)

- **List boxes** and **combo boxes** allow you to choose from lists (see page 64).

- **Drive**, **directory** and **file list boxes** are specialised list boxes for choosing files. The **Common Dialog** ActiveX control adds a standard Windows dialog box (see page 138).

- The **data** control provides access to existing databases. The **OLE** control allows you to create links to other applications. (See also Chapter 11.)

In addition to these, there are other **ActiveX controls** for performing more specialised tasks. Some of these are supplied with Visual Basic, many others are available from third-party suppliers. For example, the **Microsoft grid** control adds a spreadsheet-style display to a form. ActiveX controls are added with the Project|Components option.

Re-running the application

Try out some of these controls (examples are given over the page). You can see what your application will look like by pressing **[F5]** to run it. Clicking on a command button won't do anything but you will see the button change as it is 'depressed'. You can click on an option button, and check boxes can be switched on or off.

Always save the project before running it. Occasionally, the system may 'hang' but providing you have saved your work, this should not be a problem. Remember that you can get out of an application by switching to VB and selecting Run|End.

By this stage you should have created a fairly impressive 'front end' to your application – all without writing a line of code. Now, to make the windows and controls respond to the user's actions, you need to start adding program code.

Exercises

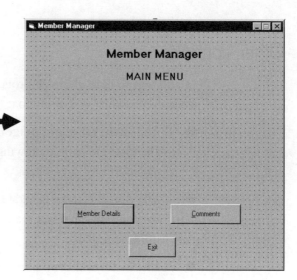

1 Add labels and command buttons to the front-end form, as shown here. The Exit button should be set up so that it is activated by pressing the **[Esc]** key.

2 Create a password form. When text is typed into the text box it should show as asterisks.

3 Add controls to the Details form.

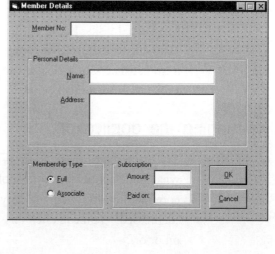

4 Add a text box and buttons to the Comments form.

5 Save all files and test the application. (At this stage only the front-end window will be displayed and the command buttons will be ineffective.)

For solutions to these exercises, see page 175.

4 Coding events

The event-led environment

In traditional programming languages, the programmer is in complete control while the program is running. The program consists of a linear sequence of coded instructions, with branches to particular points in the program. At each stage of the program, the user is offered a limited number of options and the program branches to the relevant section of code, according to the choice that has been made. If the code has been written correctly, there should be no surprises.

Windows programming languages, such as Visual Basic, start from a very different viewpoint. At any one time there will be many **objects** on the screen: windows, buttons, menus, text boxes and so on. The user is free to click, drag or type on any object and, in most circumstances, is not constrained to follow a linear path through a fixed sequence of actions.

This **event-led** environment requires the programmer to take a completely new approach. Rather than trying to confine the user to a limited number of actions, the programmer must create a program that reacts correctly to whatever the user does. This is not as daunting as it sounds; there are, of course, ways of limiting the user's scope (for example, making forms and controls invisible or greying out check boxes) but the simplest method is to do nothing.

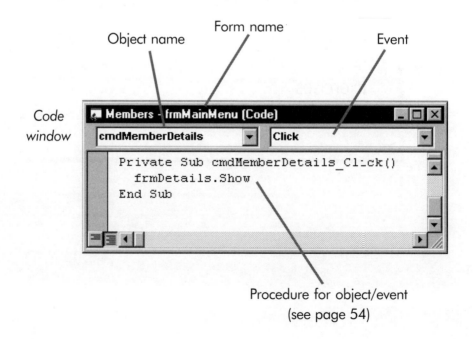

Object name — Form name — Event

Code window

```
Members - frmMainMenu (Code)
cmdMemberDetails          Click
    Private Sub cmdMemberDetails_Click()
        frmDetails.Show
    End Sub
```

Procedure for object/event
(see page 54)

For each object on the screen there are a number of possible **events**. Some of these are generated by the user: for instance, clicking or double-clicking the mouse-button, dragging an object across the screen or pressing a key. Others arise as a result of some other event occurring in the system: for example, a window opening or closing, a control getting or losing the focus, or the system time reaching some predefined value.

The code to respond to these events is contained in Visual Basic **procedures**. For any object, there is a procedure for each possible event; initially, every procedure is empty, so nothing happens when the event occurs. Theoretically, you could create a procedure for every event but in practice you will only fill in the procedures for those events that are of interest.

For example, a command button's events include being clicked, getting and losing the focus, the mouse button being pressed and released. However, you may only want to provide code for the Click event; any other events would be ignored.

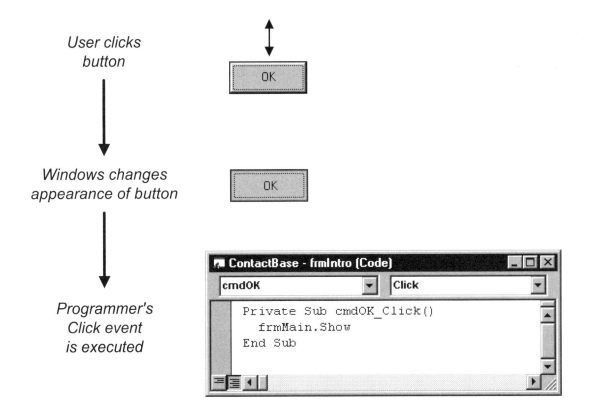

User clicks button

Windows changes appearance of button

Programmer's Click event is executed

```
Private Sub cmdOK_Click()
    frmMain.Show
End Sub
```

Each event results in some action being taken by Windows itself. For instance, clicking on a command button causes it to change its appearance while the mouse button is held down; clicking on a window's Minimise button reduces the window to an icon. In these cases, you cannot alter the object's behaviour but you can add to it; for example, you may activate a new form when the command button is clicked or display a message when a form is minimised.

Therefore, the next task, after creating the user interface, is to decide the events that are to be handled and create the appropriate procedures.

Tip

Don't try to create procedures for every possible event. For each object, look through the list of events and choose the ones that are essential. You can always add new procedures later.

Take note

The command button has a Click event but the user cannot double-click a button.

Common events

A number of events are common to most of the standard Visual Basic controls. A brief description is given here but for a full list of events select an object and then click on the Properties window. For a description of any event, search the *Events* book in the *Language Reference* (part of the *Reference* book in the *Visual Basic Documentation* section of the on-line help).

The **Click** event is generated when the user clicks the mouse button with the pointer over the object; **DblClick** occurs when the user double-clicks. For a command button or option button, the Click event is also generated if you set the Value property to True within the program; for a check box, the Click event occurs if the program makes any change to the Value property.

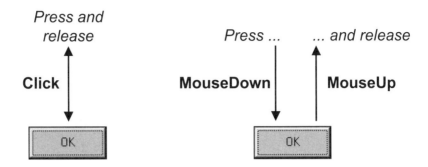

Sometimes, you may want to split the Click event into its two component parts: **MouseDown** and **MouseUp**. For instance, you may want to change the appearance of a control when the button is pressed and restore it when the button is released. You also need to use these events to find out which mouse button was pressed and whether the **[Shift]**, **[Ctrl]** or **[Alt]** keys were also pressed. (The Click event provides no extra information.)

The **MouseMove** event occurs when the pointer passes over the top of the object (useful for changing the appearance of the pointer at different places on the screen). **DragOver** occurs when an item is being dragged over the object and the **DragDrop** event is generated at the end of a drag operation when the mouse button is released. For these drag operations you can determine what object was being dragged, and take the appropriate action.

GotFocus and **LostFocus** occur when a control gets or loses the focus, respectively. GotFocus can be used to set initial values, while LostFocus is useful for checking the user's input. For example, you might use GotFocus to give an empty text box a default value and then test the user input with LostFocus; if the entry is invalid, the cursor can be put back into the text box by giving the text box the focus again (but make sure the user does not get stuck in a loop!)

In some circumstances you may want to test for keyboard activity. **KeyPress** occurs when a key is pressed; this may be split into the **KeyDown** and **KeyUp** events.

You can also find out what the user has been doing by writing a procedure for an object's **DataChanged** event. This event occurs whenever the value of a check box, label or text box changes.

Creating a procedure

Procedures are created in the **Code window**. This window is displayed either by clicking on the View Code button in the Project Explorer window or, more simply, by double-clicking on either a control or a blank part of the form. The Code window has two list boxes below the title bar:

- The **Object** box on the left shows the current object (the form or a control).

- The **Procedure** box on the right shows the event being coded.

You can choose a new object and event at any time; when you do so, the procedure code for that object and event is displayed.

Every procedure must have a name that is unique within the form. Event-driven procedures are named for you, the name consisting of the object name, an underscore and the event name. For instance, the procedure corresponding to the Click event for a command button called 'cmdExit' will be named 'cmdExit_Click'.

The procedure is written in the format:

Private Sub *object_event*()
    statements
End Sub

The first and last lines are provided for you; all you have to do is fill in the statements in the middle. When the event occurs, the procedure statements will be executed. For example, when the user clicks on the Exit button the cmdExit_Click procedure is executed.

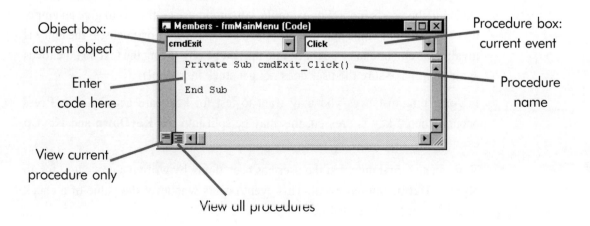

Object box: current object

Procedure box: current event

Enter code here

Procedure name

View current procedure only

View all procedures

54

Example

Using the example from the Exercises, you can set up the Member Details button on the front-end window so that, when clicked, it displays the Details form. To do this you need add only a single statement to the cmdMemberDetails_Click procedure:

1   Display the main form and double-click on the Member Details button, so that the Code window is displayed.

2   In the blank line in the middle of the procedure type:

   frmDetails.Show

   To make the procedure easier to read, start the line with two spaces.

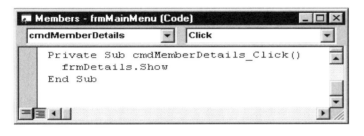

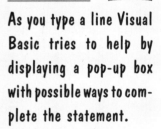

Take note

As you type a line Visual Basic tries to help by displaying a pop-up box with possible ways to complete the statement.

3   Press **[Ctrl-S]** to save the changes.

4   Press **[F5]** to run the application and then click on the Member Details button. The Details form is displayed.

5   Select End from the Visual Basic Run menu to close down the application.

Tip

Make sure that the control name is correct before you start creating procedures for it. If you rename the control later, Visual Basic will not rename the corresponding procedures — this must be done manually.

Take note

The Click event is generated by the following actions: clicking the button; tabbing to the button and pressing the spacebar; or pressing [Enter] (when Default is True).

Using and changing properties

You can make use of a control's properties when writing a procedure. You can also change most of them. The instructions to change a property must be in the format:

control.property = expression

Control is the name you have given to the object, *property* is the Visual Basic property name and *expression* is any valid Visual Basic expression (such as a piece of text or an arithmetic calculation – see page 78). The spaces around the = sign are optional.

Text properties

Properties such as Caption, Text and PasswordChar can only be assigned text expressions. The expression must consist of a text **string** (an actual piece of text in double quotes), another text property or a combination of the two. Items of text are combined using the '&' symbol.

For example, the text for a label called lblMessage can be changed with a statement such as:

```
lblMessage.Caption = "Please enter a value"
```

Any piece of text must be enclosed in a pair of double quotes. Similarly, the same message can be cleared by assigning the **null string** to the Caption:

```
lblMessage.Caption = ""
```

A text box can be given a default value with a statement such as:

```
lblCountry.Text = "UK"
```

You can refer to an existing property by including it in the expression. For example, if a name is entered in a text box, the LostFocus event for the text box could be used for displaying the name in a label as follows:

```
Private Sub txtName_LostFocus()
    lblAnswer.Caption = "Your company name is " & txtName.Text
End Sub
```

When the user tabs to another field, the label is updated.

Remember to indent the code. It can also help to insert a blank line above and below the code statements (i.e. below the Private Sub line and above End Sub).

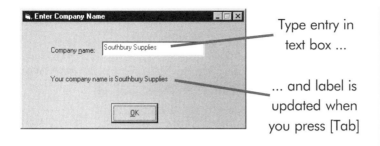

Type entry in
text box ...

... and label is
updated when
you press [Tab]

Tip

To add the procedure,
double-click on the text
box, then select LostFocus
in the Procedure box.

Numeric properties

Most properties have numeric values; for instance, Height, Width, Left, Right, BorderStyle and SmallChange are all numeric properties. These must be assigned numeric expressions, consisting of numbers and other numeric properties.

For example, the following statement changes the size of a command button:

```
cmdOK.Height = 400
cmdOK.Width = 1000
```

(Sizes are in twips – see page 20.)

A text box can be expanded or contracted to fit the inside of a resizable form as follows:

```
txtComments.Top = 0
txtComments.Left = 0
txtComments.Height = frmComments.ScaleHeight – 825
txtComments.Width = frmComments.ScaleWidth
```

Take note

The ScaleHeight and ScaleWidth properties give the internal dimensions
of the form, excluding the title bar and borders; Height and Width give
the overall dimensions. For a control, Height and Width are measured from
the middle of the control's border.

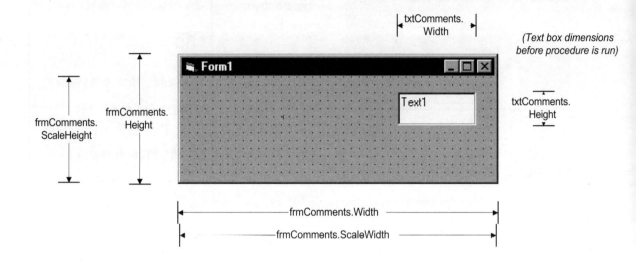

(Text box dimensions before procedure is run)

If these statements are included in the frmComments_Resize procedure, the text box will always fill the full width of the form, leaving an area at the bottom for the command buttons. The position of the command buttons can be maintained, relative to the bottom of the form, with the statements:

```
cmdOK.Top = frmComments.ScaleHeight – 600
cmdCancel.Top = cmdOK.Top
```

The horizontal positions of the buttons can be kept constant relative to the centre of the form with the statements:

```
cmdOK.Left = frmComments.ScaleWidth / 2 – 690 – cmdOK.Width
cmdCancel.Left = frmComments.ScaleWidth / 2 + 690
```

In a similar way, a form can be centred on the screen with the following statements:

```
frmFront.Left = (Screen.Width – frmFront.Width) / 2
frmFront.Top = (Screen.Height – frmFront.Height) / 2
```

These statements can be placed in the form's Load procedure, which is executed when the form is first loaded.

The use of the '/' symbol for division and the application of brackets are explained on pages 78 and 79.

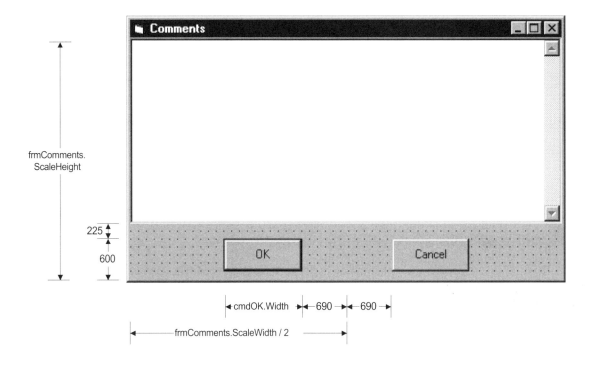

Take note

The Screen object has a few properties that tell you about the screen on which your program is being displayed.

You cannot change the Height and Width properties for the Screen object but you can use their values to change the settings for other properties.

Tip

The position of a window is not usually important, as the user is free to move it around at any time. However, it is worth setting the position of the opening screen so that it gives the right impression when first loaded. You also want to ensure that the window stays on the screen. Remember that screen size will vary from one computer to another, and some screens may have a smaller display than the machine on which the program is being developed.

Boolean properties

A number of properties can take a **Boolean** value: True or False. In such cases you can either assign values of 'True' or 'False' (without quotes) to the properties, or give them numeric values. A value of 0 (zero) is treated as False; any other value is regarded as True. (True and False are Visual Basic constants, whose numeric values are fixed. In a numeric expression, True is evaluated as –1.)

For instance, a button can be greyed out with the statement:

```
cmdPostcode.Enabled = False
```

When this statement has been executed, the button's caption will be greyed out and clicking on it will not generate a Click event.

Property references

Although most references to properties are in the form *control.property*, there are some variations.

Within an object's procedures, you can omit the control name for that object. For instance, the following two statements are identical if they appear in the procedure cmdSave_Click:

```
cmdSave.Enabled = False
Enabled = False
```

If no object is specified, the current object is assumed.

In the same way, all objects are assumed to be on the current form unless specified otherwise. You can refer to objects on other forms by prefacing the control name with the form name.

For instance, the following statement disables a button on a SaveData form:

```
frmSaveData.cmdSave.Enabled = False
```

Using the full name you can access the properties for any controls or forms included in the project.

If the statement is included in a procedure for the SaveData form or one of its controls, the form name can be omitted:

```
cmdSave.Enabled = False
```

It does no harm to include the form name and control name, even when not needed.

Methods

Each object has a number of **methods** available. These are internal procedures, which can be executed from within an event-driven procedure. The methods are used for performing some action on the object. For instance, a text box has a SetFocus method, which moves the focus to the text box.

To execute one of these methods, it must be specified in the format:

object.method

For example, if a value is required for a particular text box you can force the user to make an entry with an instruction such as:

txtCompanyName.SetFocus

As for properties and events, the methods that are available depend on the type of object.

Take note

It is important to make the distinction between properties, methods and events:

— Properties are items of information that describe a particular object (e.g. cmdOK.TabStop determines whether pressing the [Tab] key gives the button the focus).

— Methods are built-in procedures that take some action on an object (e.g. cmdOK.SetFocus gives the focus to the button).

— Events are user actions for which customised procedures may be written (e.g. cmdOK_GotFocus is executed when the button gets the focus).

Displaying forms

When you run an application, the form specified as the Startup Object is loaded into memory and displayed. Other forms can be loaded and displayed using the **Show** method. For example, the following procedure loads the Details form when the Member Details button is clicked:

```
Private Sub cmdDetails_Click()
    frmDetails.Show
End Sub
```

The start-up form

You can change the first form that is displayed when the application is run using Project| *projectname* Properties. (For Visual Basic 4.0, use Tools|Options.) Click on the General tab and select a new Startup Object from the drop-down list.

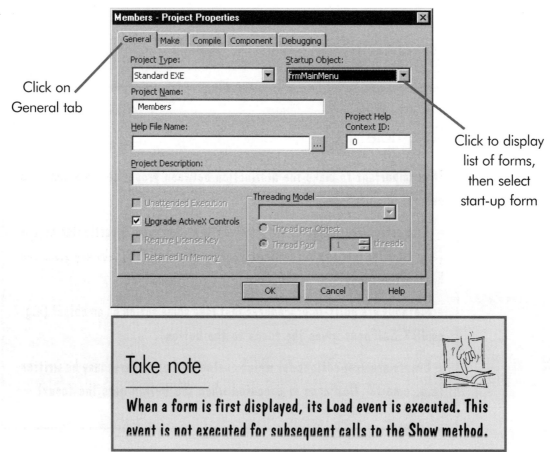

Click on General tab

Click to display list of forms, then select start-up form

Take note

When a form is first displayed, its Load event is executed. This event is not executed for subsequent calls to the Show method.

Loading and unloading forms

You can also use the **Load** statement to load a form into memory but not display it; for example:

Load frmDetails

When a form has been loaded, the Show method has the same effect as setting the Visible property to True.

A form can be hidden again with the Hide method; for example:

frmDetails.Hide

This is the same as setting the Visible property to False.

After a form has been hidden, it is still held in memory. To free the memory used by the form, use the Unload statement; for example:

Unload frmDetails

This statement removes the form from the screen, then deletes the form's data from memory. Just before a form is unloaded, its Unload event is executed. The Unload event is also executed when the window is closed in any other way: double-clicking on the Control-menu box, clicking on the Close button or selecting the Visual Basic Run|End option.

Tip

Unless you want a window to remain available to the user, include an Unload statement in the Click event for each form's 'exit' buttons (e.g. OK and Cancel). This ensures that unwanted windows are not left cluttering up the screen.

Tip.

If you unload the start-up form, the whole application should be closed down and all other forms should also be closed. (The Unload event should be executed for each one.) To make sure you catch all the possible exit points, the Unload statements for other forms should be included in the start-up form's Unload event procedure (see Exercise 3 at the end of this chapter).

Lists

Two types of control are used for selecting an item from a list. The choice of control depends on the options you want the user to have.

List boxes

The list box allows the user to select from a list of options. The box consists of a rectangle containing a list of items, with a vertical scroll bar on the right-hand side (if the list is too long to fit in the box). The size of the box is specified when you add it to the form (though you can change this by varying the Height and Width properties while the program is running).

You can specify the contents of a list box at design time using the **List** property (not available in VB 4.0).

Alternatively, items can be added to the list at run time (for example, in the form's Load procedure) using the **AddItem** method in a procedure. This takes one of the forms:

```
listbox.AddItem listitem
listbox.AddItem listitem, index
```

The *listitem* is the text item to be added to the list; *index* specifies the position for the new item in the list (starting at 0 for the item at the top of the list).

For example:

```
lstTypes.AddItem "France"
lstTypes.AddItem "Germany", 3
```

The first statement adds the item 'France' to the bottom of the list; the second statement adds 'Germany' as the fourth item in the list.

As an alternative to specifying the index number, setting the list box's **Sorted** property to True sorts the list items in alphabetical order.

When a list box has been filled:

- The **ListCount** property gives you the number of items in the list.

- The **ListIndex** property returns the index number of the item that is currently highlighted. If no item is currently selected, ListIndex is –1.

- The **Text** property contains the text of the selected item.

These properties are available only at run time.

An item can be removed from the list using the **RemoveItem** method, which takes the form:

listbox.RemoveItem *index*

For example, the following statement deletes the fourth item in a list:

lstTypes.RemoveItem 3

MultiSelect allows you to select more than one item in the list. The property can take the following settings:

0   Only a single item may be selected (the default setting).

1   Several items can be selected. Clicking on an item selects or deselects it.

2   A series of items can be selected by clicking on the first item, holding down **[Shift]** and clicking on the last item. Individual items can be selected by holding down **[Ctrl]** while clicking.

The **Columns** property sets the number of columns in the list (default 1).

If you want the list to display only whole items, set **IntegralHeight** to True; the box will be resized vertically so that it fits an exact number of items.

The procedures below illustrate the selection of a country from a list.

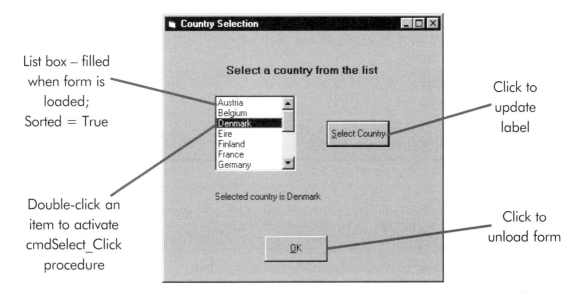

List box – filled when form is loaded;
Sorted = True

Double-click an item to activate cmdSelect_Click procedure

Click to update label

Click to unload form

65

Country selection

```
Private Sub Form_Load ()
    lstCountries.AddItem "France"
    lstCountries.AddItem "Germany"
    lstCountries.AddItem "Belgium"
    lstCountries.AddItem "Spain"
    lstCountries.AddItem "Italy"
    lstCountries.AddItem "Netherlands"
    lstCountries.AddItem "Portugal"
    lstCountries.AddItem "Greece"
    lstCountries.AddItem "Luxembourg"
    lstCountries.AddItem "Eire"
    lstCountries.AddItem "Denmark"
    lstCountries.AddItem "Austria"
    lstCountries.AddItem "Finland"
    lstCountries.AddItem "Sweden"
    lstCountries.AddItem "UK"
End Sub

Private Sub lstCountries_DblClick()
    cmdSelect_Click
End Sub

Private Sub cmdSelect_Click()
    lblChosenCountry.Caption = _
            "Selected country is " & lstCountries.Text
End Sub

Private Sub cmdOK_Click()
    Unload frmCountry
End Sub
```

> Procedure names are highlighted in bold text for ease of identification.

> The underscore character is used to split a single statement over two or more lines.

In the example, an item can be selected either by double-clicking on the item or by clicking on the item and a button. The use of a button provides a useful alternative to double-clicking. It is not a good idea to select an item with a single click, as it is very easy to click on the wrong line in a list box.

Combo boxes

A **combo box** is a combination of a text box and a list box. An item can be selected from the list either by clicking on an item or by typing an item name in the text box at the top of the control. Depending on how the combo box is set up, the user may also be able to type new values in the text box; these are then added to the list. Visual Basic uses combo boxes in a number of places: for example, the Object and Procedure boxes on the Code window are combo boxes.

The operation of a combo box is controlled by the **Style** property, which may take the following settings:

0   Clicking on the arrow makes the list drop down. An item can be selected by clicking or typing in the text box. New items can be inserted in the text box.

1   Similar to **0** but the list is displayed at all times.

2   Clicking on the arrow makes the list drop down. An item can only be selected by clicking on it.

The properties for combo boxes are similar to those for list boxes but the following points should be noted:

● For styles 0 and 1, a **Change** event is generated when the entry in the text box is edited. The **ListIndex** property is set to –1 for new entries.

● For style 2, the **DblClick** event is not valid.

Combo boxes are useful where you want to give the user the option of extending the list. They also take up less space on the form than a simple list box.

Enter a new item (Style = 0)

Click to select (Double-click if Style = 0 or 1)

Click to show list (Style = 0 or 2)

Dealing with errors

Various errors may occur while you are creating procedures and running the application.

● If you make a mistake while typing one of the instructions, so that Visual Basic cannot interpret it, an error message will be displayed when you try to move out of the line. Click on OK and the cursor will be put back in the offending line. You can either make a correction or – if you want to leave it as it is for the moment – just move out of the line again. In this way, many of your typing errors will be picked up as soon as you make them.

● If you run the application and an error is found – for example, a statement contains a reference to a form that doesn't exist – then a message box will be overlaid, specifying the nature of the error. If you click on Debug, the Code window will be displayed, with a shaded box around the error. After correcting the error, you can either continue running the program by pressing **[F5]** or end the program with Run|End.

For more information on handling errors, see Chapter 7.

Invalid line shown in different colour

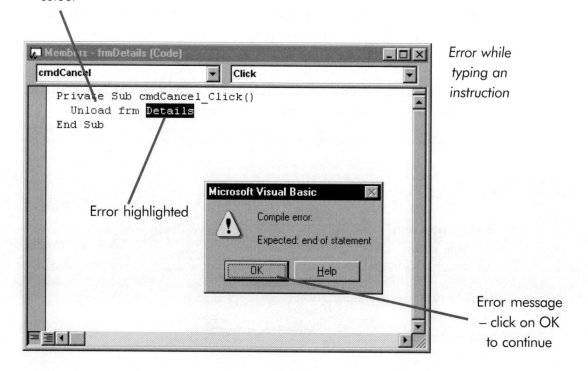

Error while typing an instruction

Error highlighted

Error message – click on OK to continue

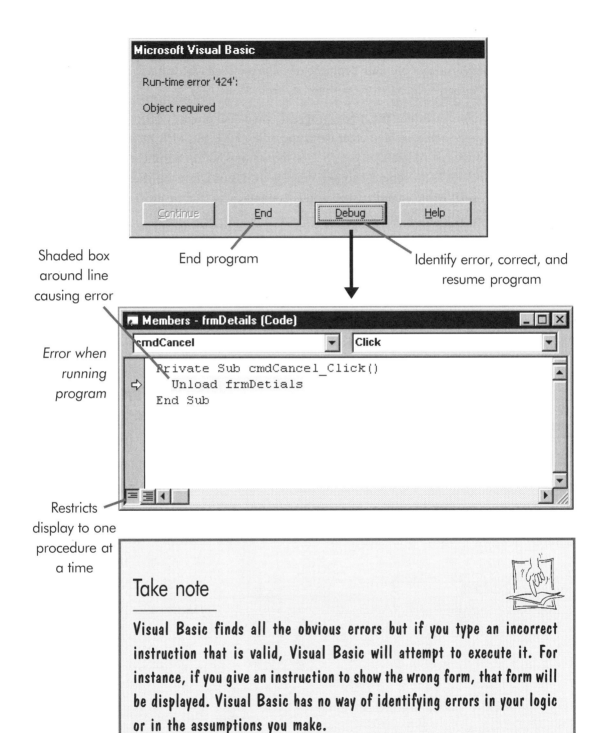

Shaded box
around line
causing error

End program

Identify error, correct, and
resume program

*Error when
running
program*

Restricts
display to one
procedure at
a time

Take note

Visual Basic finds all the obvious errors but if you type an incorrect instruction that is valid, Visual Basic will attempt to execute it. For instance, if you give an instruction to show the wrong form, that form will be displayed. Visual Basic has no way of identifying errors in your logic or in the assumptions you make.

Executable files

Up until this point, the program has been run from within Visual Basic by pressing **[F5]**. As your program begins to develop, you can also test it as a standalone EXE program (which can be run directly from Windows).

Before creating the EXE program, save the project. Then select File|Make *projectname*.exe and enter the name of the EXE file. (The name of the project is offered as a default.) If you click on the Options button, various details can be filled in, such as the version number. When you click on OK in the Make Project window, Visual Basic compiles the various components – forms, procedures etc. – into a single executable file.

You can create an icon on the desktop for this program (using the usual Windows options) and run the program without having Visual Basic running at the same time.

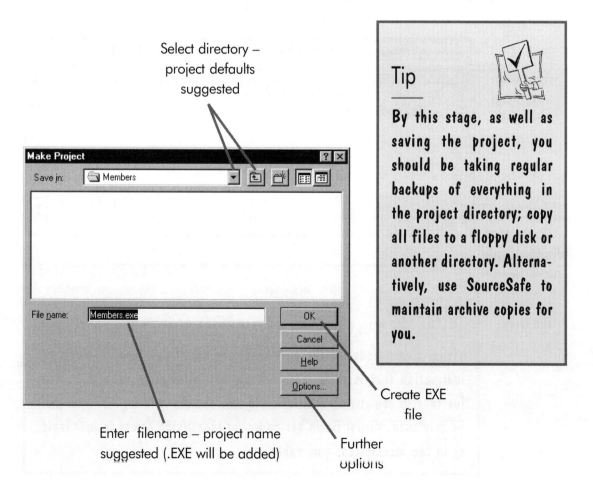

Select directory – project defaults suggested

Enter filename – project name suggested (.EXE will be added)

Create EXE file

Further options

Tip

By this stage, as well as saving the project, you should be taking regular backups of everything in the project directory; copy all files to a floppy disk or another directory. Alternatively, use SourceSafe to maintain archive copies for you.

70

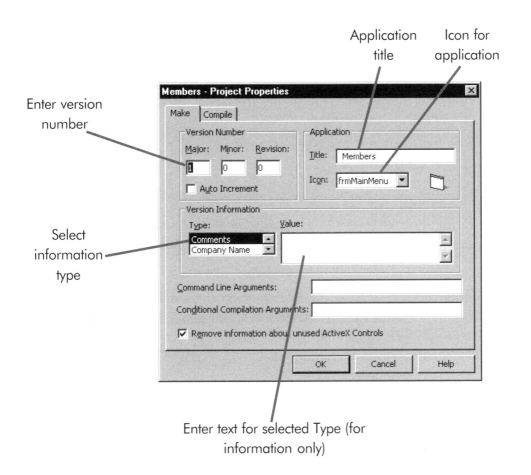

Enter version number

Application title

Icon for application

Select information type

Enter text for selected Type (for information only)

Take note

If you have made further changes to the application you can still run it by pressing [F5]; this wil not affect the EXE file. The executable version will only be updated when you choose File|Make Exe again.

Take note

If you transfer your program to another machine, you will also need to copy certain library files from the **WINDOWS\SYSTEM** directory. At the very least you will need **MSVBVM60.DLL** (or **MSVBVM50.DLL** for VB 5.0, **VBRUN400.DLL** for VB 4.0). Before copying any library file onto another machine, always make sure that there is not a more recent version already there.

Exercises

1   Using the example from the Chapter 3 Exercises, modify the Click procedure for the Member Details button on the front-end form so that it displays the Details window.

2   Modify the Click procedure for the Comments button so that it displays the Comments window.

3   Add the necessary code so that the Exit button ends the program.

4   Add suitable code to centre the front-end form when it is first loaded.

5   Add a combo box to the Details form so that the region can be selected from North, South, East and West.

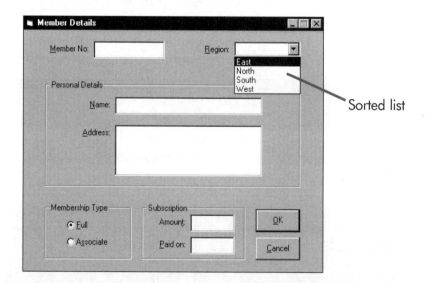

Sorted list

6   Adapt the OK and Cancel buttons on the Details form so that both return the focus to the front-end form (and unload the Details form).

7   Modify the Comments form so that the text box fills the full width of the window, leaving enough space at the bottom for the buttons.

8   Adapt the OK and Cancel buttons so that they unload the Comments form and return you to the front-end form.

For solutions to these exercises, see page 178.

5 Variables

Using variables

While an application is running, you will want to store information temporarily. For example, if a set of statements is to be processed a number of times you need to hold the repeat number and update a count each time the loop is completed; when users enter information in text boxes, this new data may have to be kept somewhere until you use it. All this information is stored in **variables**.

A variable is simply a named location in memory where a single item of data is held. Variables are created by being **declared** within a procedure or form. They can then be given values and these values can be retrieved or changed.

In the same way as for properties, variables fall into two categories:

● **Numeric variables** hold numbers (whole numbers, decimals, percentages, currency amounts and date values) and the settings for numeric properties.

● **String variables** hold items of text and the settings for text properties.

You cannot mix these two types; for instance, a numeric variable cannot hold a text string unless the string has first been converted to a number.

Variable names

Variable names must follow these rules:

● A variable name can be up to 255 characters long, consisting of letters, numbers and the underscore character.

● The name must start with a letter.

● There must be no spaces or other symbols in the name.

● Upper and lower case letters are treated as being the same.

● You must not use reserved words (names that have a special meaning within Visual Basic, such as If and Left). These are listed in the various topics under 'keywords' in the on-line help.

You should choose sensible names for your variables; programs are much more readable if names are meaningful. The aim should be to create a set of names whose content is reasonably obvious: for example, CurrentDate and AddressLine1. The use of capitals helps distinguish separate words within the name; for example, 'LastTypeToProcess' is more easily understood than the equivalent 'lasttypetoprocess'.

Declaring variables

Before you can use a variable it should be **declared**. A declaration is a statement specifying the name of a variable and its type.

Every form has a (General) object, which is at the top of the Object list in the Code window. Each (General) object has a (Declarations) section, which can be found at the top of the list in the Procedure box. This is one of the places where variables can be declared.

The point at which a variable is declared determines its **scope**: the scope of a variable affects where else in the project it may be used:

● **Local variables**, declared at the start of a procedure, are available only within that procedure.

● **Form-level variables**, declared in the (Declarations) section, are available to all procedures in the form.

Local variables are declared using the **Dim** keyword as follows:

> Dim *variable* As *type*

You can declare several variables on the same line:

> Dim *variable1* As *type1*, *variable2* As *type2*

Take note

Properties can be thought of as predefined variables attached to particular objects; the property names are equivalent to the variable names and the property settings are the variable values.

Take note

You can use the Static keyword as an alternative to Dim. The values of Static variables are remembered after you leave a procedure and will be the same when the procedure is called again; the values of variables declared with the Dim keyword are cleared (to zero for numeric variables or the null string for string variables) every time the procedure is called.

The *type* can be any of the following:

Type	Bytes	Use
Boolean	2	Values that can be either True or False
Byte	1	Whole numbers in the range 0 to 255
Integer	2	Whole numbers in the range $-32{,}768$ to $+32{,}767$
Long	4	Very large whole numbers ($\pm 2{,}000{,}000{,}000$)
Currency	8	Numbers with an exact number of decimal places (depending on your Country settings in Windows Control Panel)
Single	4	Floating-point (decimal) numbers with up to 7 significant figures
Double	8	Floating-point numbers, up to 14 sig. figs.
Date	8	Floating-point numbers representing a combined date and time
String	*	Text values
Object	4	References to objects within the application
Variant	**	Capable of holding any type of value

*	Strings require 1 byte per character
**	Variant values require 16 bytes plus 1 extra byte per character

When declaring a variable, use a type from as high in this list as possible. For instance, if you know that a value will always be a whole number, choose Integer rather than Single; if the value will always be in the range 1–100, choose Byte. The types higher in the list use less memory and programs containing them run faster.

Form-level variables are declared in the (Declarations) section using the **Private** keyword:

Private *variable* As *type*

These variables can be used by any procedure in the form. You can also use Dim instead of Private; the effect is the same.

Constants

Some variables have fixed values that cannot be changed, either by the user or a procedure. These can be declared as **constants** using the **Const** keyword.

● Constants declared in a procedure are local to that procedure.

● Constants declared in the (Declarations) section of a form are available throughout the form.

Constant declarations take the form:

Const *variable* = *value*

Constants help to make your program easier to understand. They also reduce the risk of things going wrong, since the value of a constant cannot be changed inadvertently.

Form-level
variable
declarations

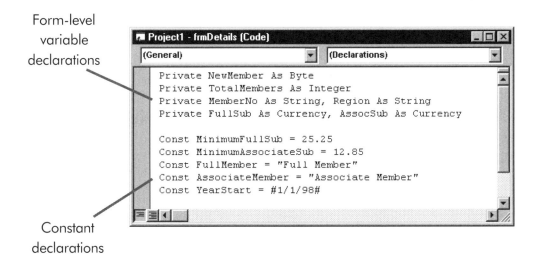

Constant
declarations

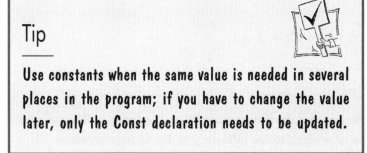

Tip

Use constants when the same value is needed in several places in the program; if you have to change the value later, only the Const declaration needs to be updated.

Take note

Dates must be enclosed in # signs when given specific values.

Expressions

Values are assigned to variables using **expressions**. Such statements take the form:

variable = expression

The expression can be either a specific value or a combination of variables and values, linked together by **operators**. For example:

StartPos = 5
EndPos = StartPos + 37

In the first case, the variable StartPos is given an explicit value of 5. In the second case, 37 is added to the value of StartPos and the result is stored in EndPos; so if StartPos is 5, EndPos will be 42. The value of the variable on the left of the expression is always changed by the statement; any variables in the expression itself are never changed.

Variables can also refer to themselves, as in this example:

StockIn = 32
CurrentStock = CurrentStock + StockIn

The value of StockIn (32) is added to the existing value of CurrentStock. So, if CurrentStock was originally 68, its value is now 100.

Numeric operators

For numeric expressions, you can combine variables and values using the following operators:

^   Raising to the power (e.g. 5 ^ 2 is 5 squared, or 25)

*   Multiplication (e.g. 6 * 7 is 42)

/   Division (e.g. 14 / 5 is 2.8)

\   Integer division (e.g. 14 \ 5 is 2)

Mod   Remainder (e.g. 14 Mod 5 is 4)

+   Addition

–   Subtraction

Where an expression contains more than one operator, the calculation is not done from left to right but according to the following **order of precedence**:

^	Raising to the power
–	Negation (when the operator starts the expression; e.g. –2)
* /	Multiplication and division
\	Integer division
Mod	Remainder
+ –	Addition and subtraction

For example:

$$137 - 6 \text{ ^ } 2 * 3 = 137 - 36 * 3 = 137 - 108 = 29$$

However, to avoid confusion, it is better to use brackets.

Brackets

Inserting brackets in an expression changes the order of calculation. Anything inside a pair of brackets is calculated first. Brackets must always be in matching pairs. Use only round brackets ( ), not square brackets [] or braces {}.

If brackets are nested – one pair inside another – the calculations start with the innermost pair of brackets and work outwards. For example:

$$8 + (3 * (10 / 2 - 3)) \text{ ^ } 2$$
$$= 8 + (3 * 2) \text{ ^ } 2$$
$$= 8 + 6 \text{ ^ } 2$$
$$= 44$$

It is usually better to split complex expressions over two or more lines.

The following program demonstrates the use of some simple expressions.

Take note

For very large or very small numbers, values are displayed in exponential form, $n.nn\text{E}\pm pp$ where $n.nn$ is in the range 1.00 to 9.99 and pp is a power of ten; e.g. 8,750 is represented by 8.75E+03 (i.e. 8.75 x 1000) and 0.000875 is 8.75E–04 (i.e. 8.75 / 10,000).

VAT Calculation

(Declarations)
```
'Declare constants for use in whole form
Const VatPercentage = 17.5
Const VatRate = VatPercentage / 100
```

Private Sub cmdCalculate_Click()

```
    'Declare local variables
    Dim NetAmount As Currency
    Dim VAT As Currency, GrossAmount As Currency

    'Get amount for calculations
    NetAmount = Val(txtNet.Text)

    'Calculate values
    VAT = NetAmount * VatRate
    GrossAmount = NetAmount + VAT

    'Put results in text boxes
    txtVAT.Text = Format(VAT, "0.00")
    txtGross.Text = Format(GrossAmount, "0.00")
```

End Sub

Private Sub cmdExit_Click()

```
    Unload frmVAT
```

End Sub

Private Sub Form_Load()

```
    'Put constant VAT percentage in VAT % box
    txtRate.Text = Str(VatPercentage)
```

End Sub

Private Sub txtNet_LostFocus()

```
    cmdCalculate_Click
```

End Sub

Anything after a single quote is a comment and is ignored by the program.

Val converts a string value to a number – see page 86.

Format specifies format for numbers – see on-line help.

Str converts a numeric value to a string – see page 85.

VAT Calculator

Net Amount: 106.23

VAT Rate: 17.5 %

VAT Amount: 18.59

Gross Amount: 124.82

Calculate   Exit

String variables and properties

Expressions can also include string variables (for handling text) and properties (both string and numeric). However, you cannot mix numeric and string variables.

String variables

String variables are much simpler to use than numeric variables. You can assign a particular item of text to a string variable by enclosing it in double quotes:

    UserCountry = "UK"

You can also combine strings. (This is called **concatenation**.) The & operator adds one string to another. For instance:

    FullName = FirstName & " " & Surname

Here, the two parts of the name are added together with a space in the middle.

Tip

Unlike other operators, it is essential to put a space on either side of the & symbol; otherwise, it will not be recognised.

Take note

You can use + instead of &; the effect is the same. However, it is better to use & to avoid ambiguity.

Properties

You can use properties in expressions in the same way as you would variables. The following statements place a text box in the middle of a form, the height of the box being provided by a variable, HistHt:

    txtHistory.Height = HistHt
    txtHistory.Top = (frmHist.ScaleHeight – HistHt) / 2

The text box can be filled by the value of a string variable, HistText, as follows:

    txtHistory.Text = HistText

Numeric expressions can only include numeric properties and string expressions can only include text properties.

Functions

Visual Basic incorporates a number of built-in **functions**. These are routines that carry out specific operations on one or more values and return a result.

The values supplied to a function are called **arguments** and are enclosed in brackets, following the function name. Multiple arguments are separated by commas. (If you do not put spaces after the commas, Visual Basic will insert them for you.)

Each argument can be a specific value or an expression. For example, the **Int** function returns the integer part of a floating-point number:

```
LengthMetres = Int(TotalLength)

NearestInt = Int(X + 0.5)
```

In the first example, the value of TotalLength is rounded down to the nearest whole number, with the answer stored in LengthMetres. In the second case, the argument is an expression and has the effect of rounding X to the nearest whole number.

Visual Basic provides many other numeric functions, including:

Abs	Absolute (positive value)
Sgn	Sign of value (returns 1 if positive, −1 if negative and 0 if zero)
Fix	Truncated value
Sqr	Square root
Log	Natural logarithm
Exp	Exponential value
Sin	Sine of angle in radians
Cos	Cosine of angle in radians
Tan	Tangent of angle in radians
Atn	Arctangent (angle whose tangent is given)

The **Rnd** function generates a random number between 0 and 1. If a negative number is given as the argument, the same sequence is generated each time. (The **Randomize** statement initialises the random number sequence.)

Various other functions are introduced in later sections and many more can be found in the Visual Basic on-line *Language Reference*.

String functions

There are also many string functions. Some of the most useful functions are those that act on one string to produce another. These include:

Left(*string*, *length*)

Returns a string of given *length* from the left-hand side of the *string*

e.g. Left("South", 2) returns 'So'

Right(*string*, *length*)

Returns a string of given *length* from the right-hand side of the *string*

e.g. Right("South", 2) returns 'th'

Mid(*string*, *start*, *length*)

Returns a string of given *length* for the specified *string*, beginning at the *start* character position; if no *length* is given, the text returned continues to the end of the string

e.g. Mid("South", 2, 3) returns 'out'

Len(*string*)

Returns the length of the *string*

e.g. Len("South") is 5

LTrim(*string*)

Removes leading spaces from *string*

e.g. LTrim(" South") is 'South'

RTrim(*string*)

Removes trailing spaces from *string*

e.g. RTrim("South ") is 'South'

Trim(*string*)

Removes spaces at both ends of the *string*

e.g. Trim(" South ") is 'South'

String(*length*, *character*)

Creates a string of the specified *character* for the given *length*

e.g. String(5, "S") returns 'SSSSS'

UCase(*string*)

Converts the *string* to capitals

e.g. UCase("South") returns 'SOUTH'

LCase(*string*)

Converts the *string* to lower case

e.g. LCase("South") returns 'south'

The programs in the remainder of this book contain many examples of these functions.

The **InStr** function allows you to search for one string within another. There may be up to three arguments for the function, which takes the form:

InStr(*start, main, search*)

The function searches the *main* string for the first occurrence of the *search* string, beginning the search at the *start* position. (Characters in the main string are numbered from 1 on the left-hand side.)

If no *start* value is given, the whole string is searched. For example, the following code extracts the surname from a text box:

```
Dim Surname As String
Dim SpacePos As Integer
SpacePos = InStr(txtFullName.Text, " ")
Surname = Mid(txtFullName.Text, SpacePos + 1)
```

The first two lines declare the variables that are used in the routine. The third line searches a text box (named txtFullName) for a space, putting the position of the space in the SpacePos variable. The final line extracts from the text box the text starting from the character after the space to the end, putting it in the string variable Surname.

Make sure that you put exactly one space between the double quotes; otherwise, the search will not be successful.

If the search string is not found, the function returns a value of 0.

Tip

Rather than using a space in a pair of double quotes (as in the example above), it is usually better to use a constant or the Chr(32) function — see page 94.

Take note

InStr is case sensitive; it distinguishes between upper and lower case letters when searching. If in doubt, use UCase to convert the main string to capitals and enter the search string in upper case as well.

String conversions

Each character in a string is represented in memory by a numeric code in the range 0 to 255. The codes used are from the **ASCII character set**. In this system, A is represented by 65, B by 66 and so on; lower-case letters start at 97, numeric digits at 48; the space character is 32. If you specify one of these codes in a string, the required character will be displayed on screen or printed.

The first 128 ASCII codes are mostly standard and should produce the same result in any character font. Codes 0–31 are used for control characters, which are often found embedded in files. The most useful control characters are 9 (tab character), 10 (line feed), 11 (form feed) and 13 (carriage return). Codes between 32 and 126 are all printable characters.

The codes for 128 onwards are rather more variable and their interpretation depends on how the computer or printer is set up and the fonts being used. These are the **extended ASCII codes**. For example, if you create a string of Greek characters on one computer they may appear as a completely different set of characters on another screen or when printed.

For this reason, the extended characters are best avoided unless you are contolling the fonts that are used. Remember that you may have to supply users with any unusual fonts you are using.

The **Chr** function returns the character whose ASCII code is given; for example, Chr(32) returns a space. The reverse of this is the **Asc** function, which converts a character to its ASCII code. So Chr(74) is 'J' and Asc("J") is 74. Examples are given below.

Take note

Two characters that may cause problems are 35 (which can appear as # or £, depending on the device selected) and 127 (the Delete control character).

Variable conversions

As we have seen, Visual Basic makes a very clear distinction between numeric and string variables. Two functions, Str and Val, convert values from one format to the other.

Str converts a number (or the contents of a numeric variable or expression) to a string. The following code assumes that HouseNum is a numeric variable and StreetName is a string:

```
Dim HouseNumS As String, FullAddress As String
HouseNumS = Trim(Str(HouseNum))
FullAddress = HouseNumS & Chr(32) & StreetName
```

If HouseNum has the value 23 and StreetName is 'High Street', the contents of FullAddress will be '23 High Street'.

The **Val** function reverses this process, converting a string to a numeric value. The function uses as much of the string as it can, up to the first non-numeric character, ignoring spaces. Using the example above, Val(FullAddress) would return 23.

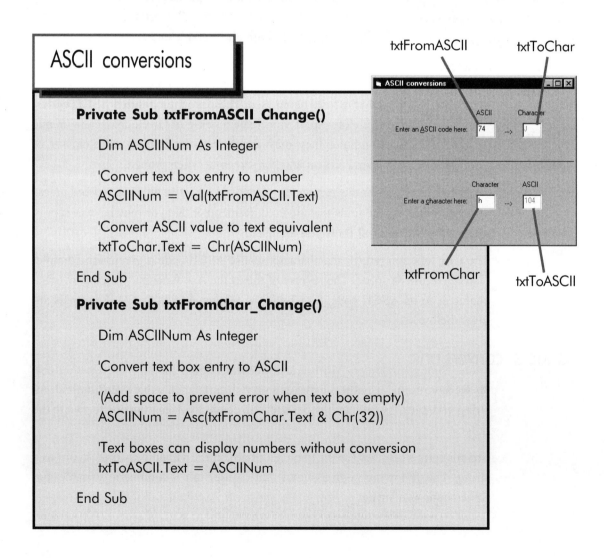

ASCII conversions

Private Sub txtFromASCII_Change()

    Dim ASCIINum As Integer

    'Convert text box entry to number
    ASCIINum = Val(txtFromASCII.Text)

    'Convert ASCII value to text equivalent
    txtToChar.Text = Chr(ASCIINum)

End Sub

Private Sub txtFromChar_Change()

    Dim ASCIINum As Integer

    'Convert text box entry to ASCII

    '(Add space to prevent error when text box empty)
    ASCIINum = Asc(txtFromChar.Text & Chr(32))

    'Text boxes can display numbers without conversion
    txtToASCII.Text = ASCIINum

End Sub

Dates and times

The Date variable type holds a floating-point number that represents a combined date and time. The integer part of the number returns the date, representing the number of days since 30-Dec-1899. Therefore 1 represents 31-Dec-1899, 2 is 1-Jan-1900 and 36526 is 1-Jan-2000. Negative numbers give you dates before 30-Dec-1899 (and are accurate back to 1752, when the Gregorian calendar was introduced).

Take note

This is the same system that is used on Excel, Lotus 1-2-3 and other spreadsheet programs. However, some versions of Excel and Lotus are inaccurate for dates before 1-Mar-1900 and will produce different results to Visual Basic.

Excel and Lotus do not allow negative dates. Excel 95 stops at 31-Dec-2078 (65380) while Lotus continues to 31-Dec-2099 (73050); dates in Visual Basic and later versions of Excel go on to the year 9999.

The decimal part of the date/time value represents the time as a proportion of the day. For instance, 6 a.m. is represented by 0.25, midday is 0.5 and midnight is 0.

The combination of the two numbers gives a complete date and time; so 36526.25 represents 1-Jan-2000 6:00 a.m.

The **Day**, **Month** and **Year** functions extract appropriate values from a date/time value. Similarly, **Hour**, **Minute** and **Second** extract the relevant time values. **Weekday** returns a number representing the day of the week (by default, 1 for Sunday, 2 for Monday etc.)

DateValue converts a string to a date value; for example, DateValue("31 Dec, 1999") returns the date '31/12/99'. Similarly, **TimeValue** converts a string to a time value; for instance, TimeValue("6:00 PM") and TimeValue("18:00") both return the time '18:00:00'. DateValue etc. return date/time variables. If you display these in text boxes, their string representations are shown. However, in calculations they are treated as numbers. **DateSerial** and **TimeSerial** return similar values but take three arguments: year, month and day, or hour, minute and second. To get the same values as the previous examples you could use DateSerial(1999, 12, 31) and TimeSerial(18, 0, 0). Use DateValue and TimeValue when dealing with text strings entered by the user or derived from some other source; use DateSerial and TimeSerial where the separate date/time components are available.

The **Date** and **Time** functions return date/time values representing the current system date and time respectively; **Now** returns a single value representing both date and time. There are no arguments to these functions.

The following program converts a date/time value to a real date and gives the day of the week; it also calculates the date/time value for a real date and adds or subtracts a given number of days to give a second date.

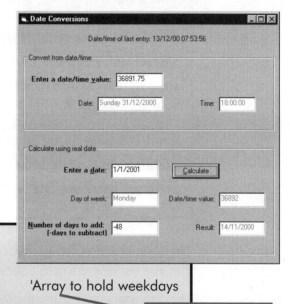

Date conversions

(Declarations)
    Dim WeekDayString(7) As String   'Array to hold weekdays

Private Sub Form_Load()
    WeekDayString(1) = "Sunday"   'Set up weekdays array
    WeekDayString(2) = "Monday"
    'ADD LINES for Tuesday to Saturday (3 to 7)
End Sub

Private Sub txtDateTimeIn_Change()
    Dim DateIn As Date, DayNumber As Integer
    Dim DateString As String, DayOfWeek As String
    Dim HourString As String, MinString As String
    Dim SecString As String, TimeString As String

See page 90 for a description of arrays.

```
        Const sl = "/"          'Constants for creating strings
        Const sp = " ": Const zr = "00": Const cn = ":"

        DateIn = Val(txtDateTimeIn.Text)  'Get day of week
        DayNumber = WeekDay(DateIn)
        DayOfWeek = WeekDayString(DayNumber)

        'Extract date components and create date string
        DateString = Day(DateIn) & sl & Month(DateIn) _
                                & sl & Year(DateIn)
        txtDate.Text = DayOfWeek & sp & DateString

        'Extract time components and create time string
        HourString = Right(zr & Hour(DateIn), 2)   'Pad with 0s
        MinString = Right(zr & Minute(DateIn), 2)
        SecString = Right(zr & Second(DateIn), 2)
        TimeString = HourString & cn & MinString & cn & SecString
        txtTime.Text = TimeString
        'Update date/time label
        lblNow.Caption = "Date/time of last entry: " & Str(Now)
End Sub

Private Sub cmdCalculate_Click()
        Dim DateNumber As Date, ResultDateNumber As Date
        Dim DayNumber As Integer
        'Calculate date/time value
        DateNumber = DateValue(txtDateIn.Text)
        txtDateTime.Text=Format(DateNumber, "#####")
        'Calculate day of week
        DayNumber = WeekDay(DateNumber)
        txtDayOfWeek.Text = WeekDayString(DayNumber)
        'Calculate value for Result box
        ResultDateNumber = DateNumber + Val(txtAddDays.Text)
        txtResult.Text = Format(ResultDateNumber, "dd/mm/yyyy")
        'Update date/time label
        lblNow.Caption = "Date/time of last entry: " & Str(Now)
End Sub
```

> Continue statement on next line.

> The Format function specifies the output appearance.

Arrays

When handling many values or strings, the use of simple variables can be rather cumbersome. For instance, if you want to hold the values to fill a large list box you do not want a separate variable for each item, nor do you want a separate statement for adding each item to the list. You can overcome these problems by the use of arrays.

An **array** is a set of variables, represented by a single name. The individual values are called **elements** and are identified by **index numbers**. The index number is given in brackets after the name.

For example, the array MonthDays could hold the number of days in the month; MonthDays(1) holds the number of days in January, MonthDays(2) is for February and so on to MonthDays(12), which represents the number of days in December.

Arrays are declared in the same way as for variables. You must declare the type of the array and, within the brackets, specify the largest index number. For example:

    Dim MonthDays(12) As Integer

This statement declares an array of 13 elements (numbered from 0 to 12), each of which can hold an integer value.

By default, the first index number is 0. However, if you do not use index 0 in any of your arrays you can set the start number to 1 using the statement:

    Option Base 1

You can also set the minimum and maximum index numbers for each array separately. For example:

    Dim MonthDays(1 to 12) As Integer
    Dim YearInvoices(1980 To 2001) As Integer

The first statement declares an array of 12 elements (numbered from 1 to 12), each of which can hold an integer value; the second statement declares an array of 22 integers, with a variable for each year from 1980 to 2001.

An array may have more than one **dimension**. For example:

    Dim MaxTemp(1 To 12, 1 To 31) As Single

Each possible combination of the two index numbers identifies a different element. In this case there are 372 single-precision values in the array, which can be used for storing the maximum temperature in each day of the year. For instance, MaxTemp(4, 17) could hold the value for 17 April. Some elements, such as MaxTemp(11, 31), will never be used.

Any element in an array can be used in an expression in the same way as for a normal variable. The *Dates conversions* program on page 88 gives an example of an array for holding the days of the week.

The example below changes a label's caption, depending on the item selected from a combo box.

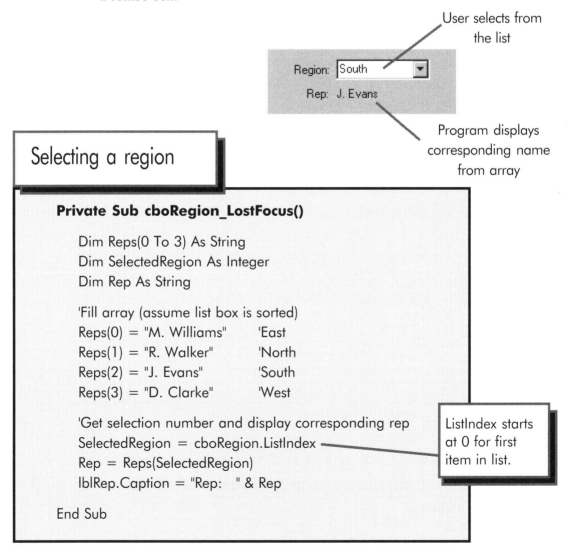

User selects from the list

Program displays corresponding name from array

Selecting a region

```
Private Sub cboRegion_LostFocus()

    Dim Reps(0 To 3) As String
    Dim SelectedRegion As Integer
    Dim Rep As String

    'Fill array (assume list box is sorted)
    Reps(0) = "M. Williams"      'East
    Reps(1) = "R. Walker"        'North
    Reps(2) = "J. Evans"         'South
    Reps(3) = "D. Clarke"        'West

    'Get selection number and display corresponding rep
    SelectedRegion = cboRegion.ListIndex
    Rep = Reps(SelectedRegion)
    lblRep.Caption = "Rep:  " & Rep

End Sub
```

ListIndex starts at 0 for first item in list.

Control arrays

You can create arrays of controls, providing a means of placing a number of similar controls on the window from within the program. When you try to duplicate a control by copying it with **[Ctrl-C]** and then pasting it with **[Ctrl-V]**, you are asked if you want to create a control array. Clicking on Yes creates a second, identical control with the same Name but an Index setting of 1. (The original has an Index of 0.)

You could add all the controls manually but for a large number of controls it is easier to use a Load statement. In this case, you should start with a single control and change its Index to 0; then use the program to load the rest of the array. An example is given on page 116.

Message boxes

A particularly useful function, **MsgBox**, displays a temporary dialog box. The box contains a line of text and one or more command buttons. The function is invoked with a statement in the following format:

$variable = MsgBox(message, features, title)$

The *message* is any line of text; *title* is the text to be displayed on the title bar; and *features* is a value indicating the number of buttons, icon type and default button. The *features* value is the sum of three numbers, one from each of the following columns:

Buttons		Icon		Default	
0	OK	0	No icon	0	1st button
1	OK, Cancel	16	Critical Message	256	2nd button
2	Abort, Retry, Ignore	32	Warning Message	512	3rd button
3	Yes, No, Cancel	48	Warning Message		
4	Yes, No	64	Information Message		
5	Retry, Cancel				

The value returned to the *variable* indicates the button that was pressed, as follows:

1	OK	5	Ignore
2	Cancel (or Esc key)	6	Yes
3	Abort	7	No
4	Retry		

For example:

$ButtonVal = MsgBox("Replace file?", 289, "Replace")$

A dialog box is displayed, with a warning icon and OK and Cancel buttons (Cancel is the default). ButtonVal is returned with a value of 1 for OK or 2 for Cancel.

Alternatively, if the key press is unimportant, you can use the MsgBox statement:

$MsgBox$ *message, features, title*

The effect is the same as for the function.

Exercises

1   Create the conversion form below. When one of the buttons is clicked the value in the left-hand box should be converted into the new units and shown in the right-hand box, to two decimal places.

The labels to the right of the boxes should be changed to show the two conversion units. When a new entry is started, the labels should be blanked out and the right-hand box should be cleared.

The Exit button should end the program.

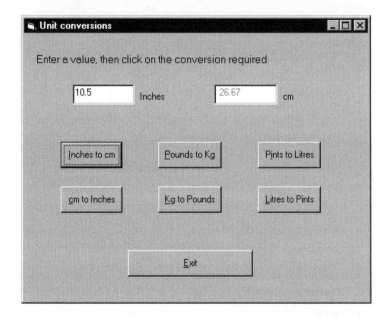

2   Add a Rep label to the Member Details form (as described in *Arrays* on page 90). Amend the code so that the program does not crash if you tab out of the Region box without making a selection.

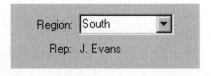

3   Write a program to calculate the number of weeks and days between any two dates.

For solutions to these exercises, see page 180.

6 Basic instructions

Modules

Much of the work done by an application is performed by event-driven procedures; these provide the responses to the user's actions. However, some code will be needed for more general-purpose actions, such as reading data from a file or checking that a date is valid. This code is put in a code **module**.

A module is a separate file that contains a collection of general-purpose procedures, which are available throughout the application. Procedures within modules are called **module-level** procedures; those in forms are **form-level**. There is no particular order to a module's procedures and they will be listed alphabetically in the Procedure box.

Most applications will have at least one code module, containing procedures for performing frequently-used tasks. These procedures are called as and when needed. This has a number of advantages:

- The code has to be written only once; when it has been tested satisfactorily you will be able to use it elsewhere in the application without having to go through the coding process again.

- Since there is only one copy of the code, there is no danger that the same process somewhere else in the application will work in a slightly different way.

- If you need to make a change to the way a procedure works, this has to be done only once; there is no need to search through your program looking for other occurrences of the same code.

- Code modules can be re-used by other applications; when you have developed a set of general-purpose procedures, these can be incorporated in other projects, helping to give all your applications the same 'look and feel'.

You can have any number of code modules in your project so it is a good idea to split up your general-purpose procedures. For instance, you may have one module for text-handling procedures, another for date routines and a third for dealing with graphics.

If you decide that part of a form procedure will be useful elsewhere, you can move it to a code module using cut-and-paste operations.

Scope

When designing the overall structure of your application it is essential to have an understanding of the **scope** of procedures. This determines what procedures are available in any part of the application. The rules are as follows:

● Any module-level procedure can call any other module-level procedure, from any module in the project (but cannot call any form-level procedures).

● Any form-level procedure can call any procedure in the same form or any module-level procedure (but not any procedures in other forms).

This is illustrated below.

You can declare a module-level procedure as **Private**, rather than Public, in which case it is available only to other procedures within that module.

Note that procedures in forms and modules can refer to any control property providing you specify the form name. See page 103 for more information on the scope of variables.

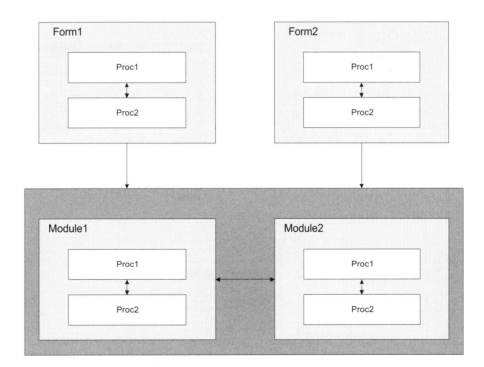

Creating modules and procedures

New modules and procedures are created with a few simple commands.

Creating modules

To create a new code module:

1   Select Project|Add Module and double-click on the Module icon. (For Visual Basic 4.0, use Insert|Module.) The Code window for the new module is displayed.

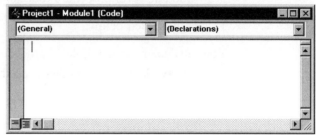

2   Select File|Save Module1 As to save the module. Enter a valid filename and click on OK; a BAS extension will be added to the name.

Enter a filename
(BAS extension
will be added)

Indicates that
only BAS files
are listed above

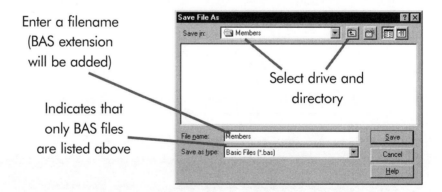

Select drive and
directory

3   The New Module is added to the Project Explorer window.

View Code

New module –
change Name
in Properties
window

Highlighting the module name in the Project Explorer window and then clicking on the View Code button redisplays the Code window.

Changing modules

You can add an existing module to the project with Project|Add Module. Click on the Existing tab and select a file with a BAS extension.

To remove a module, click on its name in the Project Explorer window and then select Project|Remove *modulename*.

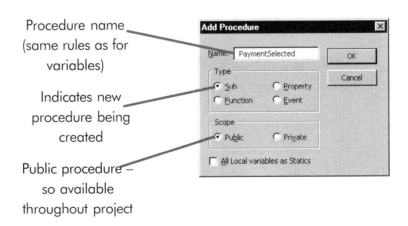

> **Take note**
>
> **Removing a module from the project does not affect the BAS file; that will still exist in the project directory.**

Creating procedures in modules

To add a general-purpose procedure to a code module:

1   Double-click on the module name in the Project Explorer window (or click on the module and then on the View Code button). The Code window is displayed.

The only 'object' for a code module is called '(General)'. This is because there are no visible objects for the module (such as buttons and lists) and therefore no events.

2   Select Tools|Add Procedure from the menu bar. (For VB 4.0, use Insert|Procedure.) The Add Procedure window appears.

Procedure name
(same rules as for
variables)

Indicates new
procedure being
created

Public procedure –
so available
throughout project

3   Enter a name for the procedure (following the rules given below) and click on OK.

4   The new procedure is displayed in the Code window, with the Sub and End Sub lines supplied. You can now type in the code for the procedure, between these two lines.

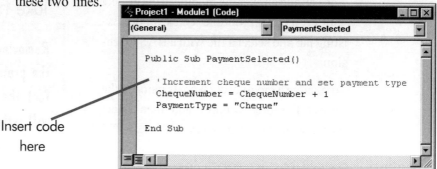

Insert code
here

The procedure can be viewed or edited later simply by selecting it from the Procedure drop-down list in the Code window.

Creating procedures in forms

You can also add a general-purpose procedure to a form. This is achieved in a similar way to that for module-level procedures:

1   Click on the form name in the Project Explorer window, then on the View Code button.

2   In the Object box, instead of selecting one of the controls or the form itself, choose '(General)'. Any existing general-purpose procedures are listed by clicking on the Procedure box.

(General) object
for form

Variable and
constant declarations
for form

Click to
view all
procedures
in form

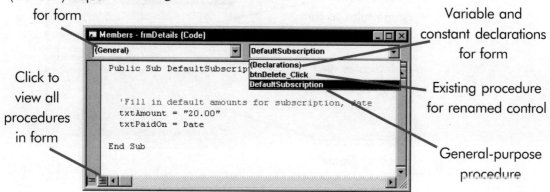

Existing procedure
for renamed control

General-purpose
procedure

3   The Tools|Add Procedure option lets you add a new procedure in the same way as before.

Form-level procedures are useful for routines that may be used more than once in a form but remember that form-level procedures cannot be used by any other form or code module.

Take note

You can only add general-purpose procedures to the (General) object; all other objects can only have event procedures attached.

Procedure names

Event procedures are automatically named for you. Their names are not necessarily unique in the project as a whole; for example, if two forms each have a cmdOK

Tip

For modules that will be used in several projects, you can avoid clashes in procedure names by starting each name with the same word. For instance, all procedures in a date-handling module could begin 'Date', while text-manipulation procedures in another module could all start 'Text'.

Take note

If you change the name of a control, its event procedures will not be renamed. Instead, they become (General) procedures. These procedures can still be used. Alternatively, they can be deleted; mark the whole procedure (including the Sub and End Sub lines) and press the [Del] key.

command button, then both will have a cmdOK_Click procedure. However, this is not a problem, since the procedures can only be called from within their own forms.

On the other hand, each general-purpose procedure in a project must be given a unique name.

The rules for naming procedures are the same as those for variables: no more than 255 characters; starting with a letter; no spaces or symbols apart from the underscore.

Use capital letters to identify individual words within the name; this helps to make the name meaningful.

Calling procedures

A general-purpose procedure is executed by **calling** it from another procedure. The procedure is called by entering the name on a line on its own in the code.

For example, a procedure called FillWidthDefaults may be used to fill the boxes on a form with default values:

```
Public Sub FillWidthDefaults()
    frmMain.txtDiscountRate.Text = "0.10"
    'Use public variable, NextInvoiceNumber
    frmMain.txtInvoiceNumber.Text = NextInvoiceNumber
End Sub
```

This procedure could be called either as part of the form's Load event or when a Defaults button is pressed on the form.

The event procedures would be as follows:

```
Public Sub Form_Load()
    FillWithDefaults
End Sub

Public Sub cmdDefaults_Click()
    FillWithDefaults
End Sub
```

In both cases, the effect is the same.

Take note

Remember that, within a module, any references to controls must specify the form name.

Public and passed variables

When you call an event-driven procedure, no other information is needed for the procedure to be executed. However, for general-purpose procedures, you usually need to make further details available to it and the procedure will often need to pass back some result. For instance, a procedure to calculate the number of days between two dates needs to know the dates to be used in the calculation and must be able to return the answer; if a procedure is used for setting up an array, the contents of the array must be made available to other procedures. All this is handled by the use of public variables and by passing the contents of variables to and from procedures.

Public variables

Variables declared in a procedure (with a Dim statement) are local to that procedure – they have no meaning elsewhere in the project. Form-level variables declared in the (Declarations) section (with a Private statement) are available throughout the form – but not in other forms or modules.

Modules also have a (Declarations) section where variables can be declared. The declarations take the following forms:

Private *variable* As *type*

Public *variable* As *type*

The **private** variables are available throughout the module but not in other modules or forms.

The **public** variables are available throughout the whole project. The value of a public variable can be used by any procedure, in any form or module. For example, a user name entered on one window may be needed elsewhere in the program, so its value must not be lost.

As a general rule, you should make variables as local as possible; use local variables in preference to private (form-level or module-level) variables, and private variables in preference to public variables. This reduces memory requirements and helps you to keep track of your variables and their values.

Public constants

Constants can also be declared in the (Declarations) section of a module. These are available to all procedures in the module.

You can also make constants **public**, making their values accessible to all procedures in the project:

> Public Const *variable* = *value*

For example:

> Public Const ProgVersion = "1.4"
> Public Const StartYear = 1997

These statements can be included in the (Declarations) section of any module.

Passing variables to procedures

One way of exchanging information with procedures would be to hold the values in public variables. However, it is more efficient to **pass** the values across when the procedure is called. The variables that are passed to the procedure must be declared in the Sub statement, in the brackets following the procedure name. The first line of the procedure will be as follows:

> Public Sub *procname* (*variable* As *type*, ...)

The brackets can contain more than one variable (when more than one value is passed). If no variables are passed, the brackets are empty. The brackets should also contain any variables that are to be passed back to the calling procedure.

When the procedure is called the variable values are listed after the procedure name. For example, the following procedure extracts the house name or number from the first line of an address:

```
Public Sub ExtractHouse(HouseName As String, StreetName As String)
    Dim CommaPos As Integer
    CommaPos = InStr(StreetName, ",")      'Find comma
    'Get house name/no. from left of street name
    HouseName = Left(StreetName, CommaPos - 1)
    'Remove house from street
    StreetName = Trim(Mid(StreetName, CommaPos + 1))
End Sub
```

Here, StreetName is used for passing a value to the procedure; the procedure uses HouseName for passing a value back and it also changes StreetName, passing back a different value.

CommaPos is a local variable, which exists only while the procedure is running.

By including variables in the Sub line you are effectively declaring them as local variables for that procedure. If you want to stop a variable being changed when passed back from a procedure, include the ByVal keyword before the variable name in the procedure definition: e.g. FillArray(ByVal Count As Integer). Here, any change to Count will not be passed back to the calling procedure.

The following procedure, which is invoked by clicking on a button, gets the contents of a text box and calls the ExtractHouse procedure. The returned values are copied into two text boxes.

```
Private Sub cmdExtract_Click()
    Dim House As String
    Dim Street As String
    Street = txtAddressLine1.Text      'Get first line of address
    ExtractHouse House, Street    'Call procedure to extract house
    txtStreet.Text = Street                'Put results back into boxes
    txtHouse.Text = House
End Sub
```

The variables that appear on the line calling the procedure do not have to have the same names as those used within the procedure itself (though they may be the same, if you wish). In the example above, the original value is passed across in the Street variable; the procedure transfers this into the corresponding StreetName local variable, which is then changed; the new value of StreetName is passed back into the Street variable. Similarly, HouseName is passed back as House.

Comments and spacing

You can make your programs more readable by adding **comments**. Although you may understand now what your program does, a few reminders might be helpful when you come to look at it again in a few months' time. On a line, any text following a single quote is treated as a comment and is ignored by Visual Basic. Therefore, you can add comments on lines of their own or at the ends of lines.

Programs are also easier to understand if they are well spaced out. Visual Basic adds spaces in each line for you but extra blank lines between sections of code help to make it clearer.

User-defined functions

Visual Basic provides many built-in functions for handling text and numbers but there will be others that you must create yourself. One way of doing this would be to use a procedure. For example, the following procedure converts inches to centimetres:

```
Public Sub InchesToCmP(Inches As Single, Cm As Single)

    Const CmPerInch = 2.54
    Cm = (Int((Inches * CmPerInch * 100) + 0.5)) / 100

End Sub
```

The converted value can be displayed in a text box with the following code:

```
InchesToCmP Inches, Cm
txtResult.Text = Cm
```

However, it is often simpler to define your own function.

User-defined functions are created in a similar way to procedures. Select Tools|Add Procedure but click on Function rather than Sub. The first and last lines of the function code are displayed. Inside the brackets you must specify any variables being passed to the function. You must also add a declaration of the function type at the end of the line.

The function code itself is inserted above the End Function line. The function returns a single value, which is calculated in a variable with the same name and type as the function.

Function name (same rules as for variables)

Indicates new function being created

Public function – so available throughout project

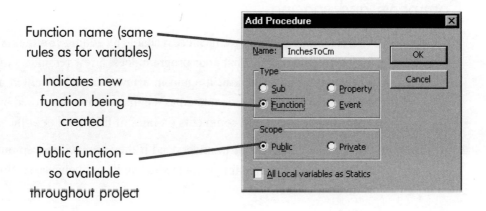

In order to use the function, include it in a statement in the same way as for a built-in function.

For example, the following function converts inches to centimetres:

```
Public Function InchesToCm(Inches As Single) As Single

    Const CmPerInch = 2.54
    InchesToCm = (Int((Inches * CmPerInch * 100) + 0.5)) / 100

End Function
```

This function could be used to supply the value for a text box, named txtResult, as follows:

```
txtResult.Text = InchesToCm(Inches)
```

When this statement is executed, the InchesToCm function is called and the value of Inches is passed to it. The function calculates the value in centimetres using the passed Inches value and the CmPerInch constant, defined in the function. The calculated value is held in the InchesToCm variable (defined as Single in the function header).

The calculated value is then slotted back into the original expression and hence into the text box's Text property.

Tip

Use a function when just one value is to be returned to the calling procedures; use a procedure when two or more values are returned, or when there are no return values.

Take note

In the same way as for procedures, several variables can be passed to a function. The types of the variables passed to the function must be an exact match for those defined in the function header.

Conditional statements

So far, the statements in a procedure have followed a linear, unbroken path; the program starts at the first line and works down through each line in turn until the last line has been completed.

Procedures are rarely like this, however. Most of the time there are choices to be made and, as a result, statements to be executed only **if** a condition is true. For example, if a value entered in a text box exceeds some limit you may want to display an error message.

Such decisions are made using the **If...Then...End If** set of statements, which take the form:

```
If condition Then
     statements
End If
```

The *statements* are executed only if the *condition* is true. The condition usually takes the form:

```
expression operator expression
```

Any valid expressions can be used, with the restriction that both must be numeric or both text; you cannot mix the two types.

The **operator** is one of the following:

=	Equal to
<>	Not equal to
<	Less than
<=	Less than or equal to
>	Greater than
>=	Greater than or equal to

For example, the following procedure tests the value of an entry in a text box when the focus is moved to another control. If the value is too high, it is replaced by the maximum allowed, a warning message is displayed and the cursor is put back in the text box.

```
Private Sub txtMinutes_LostFocus()
    If Val (txtMinutes.Text) > 59 Then
        lblWarning.Caption = "Minutes cannot exceed 59"
        txtMinutes.Text = "59"
        txtMinutes.SetFocus
    End If
End Sub
```

You do not have to indent the statements between the If and End If statements but it makes the code much more readable if you do. Indenting conditional sections of code becomes important when you start to put one condition inside another.

Take note

If you are only executing one statement, this can be put immediately after 'Then', on the same line. For example:

If TotalTime < 30 Then PayRate = 1

There is no need for an End If statement in such cases.

For numeric conditions, the tests are carried out on the relative numeric values of the expressions. For string expressions, the comparisons are performed character-by-character, according to the ASCII code of the characters. The following conditions are all true:

Numeric	String
-4 < 21	"B" < "Ba"
5 < 2^3	"B" < "a"
2.1 < 20	"2" < "B"
3 < 21	"21" < "3"

Tip

To sort strings containing numbers into numerical order, pad the numbers with leading zeroes or spaces.

Logical operators

You can combine conditions with the following **logical operators**:

And   Both conditions must be true for the combined condition to be true

Or   One (or both) of the conditions must be true

Xor   One of the conditions must be true but not both (Exclusive Or)

Eqv   Both conditions must be true or both false (Equivalence)

Imp   Either the first condition must be false or the second condition true

The two sets of conditions can be either numeric or text, independently of each other.

For example:

```
DaysInFeb = 28
If NumMonth = 2 And LeapYearTxt = "Yes" Then
    DaysInFeb = 29
End If
```

In this case, if NumMonth is not equal to 2 or LeapYearTxt contains text other than 'Yes', the value of DaysInFeb would remain at 28.

You can also negate a condition by putting **Not** in front of it. The Not operator is applied first, followed by the other logical operators in the order given above (for example, And operators are implemented before Or).

Tip

Using brackets, you can combine as many conditions as you like into a single If statement. However, to avoid any possibility of confusion, it is better to break up complex conditions using brackets or split them into a series of related If statements.

The Else statement

The conditional statements can provide alternatives for when the condition is false by including an **Else** statement, as follows:

```
If condition Then
    true_statements
Else
    false_statements
End If
```

If the *condition* is true, the *true_statements* are executed; otherwise, the *false_statements* are performed. For example:

```
If LeapYearTxt = "Yes" Then
    DaysInFeb = 29
Else
    DaysInFeb = 28
End If
```

The use of Else allows you to provide two alternative sets of statements, only one of which will ever be executed.

Nested Ifs

For complex conditions you can **nest** the If statements. For instance:

```
If NumMonth >= 1 And NumMonth <= 12 Then
    lblMonth.Caption = MonthName(NumMonth)
    lblDays.Caption = DaysInMonth(NumMonth)
    If NumMonth = 2 And LeapYearTxt = "Yes" Then
        lblDays.Caption = 29
    End If
Else
    lblMonth.Caption = "ERROR"
    lblDays.Caption = ""
End If
```

This illustrates the importance of indenting within If statements. It is clear from the indents that the statement lblDays.Caption = 29 will only be executed if both sets of conditions are true.

Case statements

When you are choosing between a number of alternatives, the **Case** statement is more appropriate than the If statement. The structure for a Case statement is as follows:

```
Select Case expression
    Case test1
        statements1
    Case test2
        statements2
    ...
    Case Else
        statementsN
End Select
```

Take note

The Case Else section is not essential, but it lets you mop up any missing values. The End Select statement must always be included, however.

The *expression* is evaluated and the result is compared against the various test values. If the expression evaluates to *test1*, then *statements1* are executed; if it is *test2*, *statements2* are executed; and so on. If none of the tests matches the expression, the final set of statements (*statementsN*) is executed.

The tests for each case can be any of the following:

● A number or numeric expression (e.g. 7, sqr(A))

● A string or string expression (e.g. "Yes", UserName)

● A range of values (e.g. 2 To 6, "A" To "AZ")

● A comparative value (e.g. Is > 6, Is < "M")

You can also combine any of these, separating them with commas; for example:

```
Case 3, 6 To 8, Is > 12
```

Here, the corresponding code is executed if the expression evaluates to 3, 6, 7, 8 or a value greater than 12.

The most important thing to remember is that the expression and the tests must be all numeric or all string.

An example is given opposite.

Identify call type

```
Private Sub txtTelNum_LostFocus()

    Dim DialCode As String

    'Get first five characters of telephone number
    'Remove leading spaces, pad to at least 5 characters
    DialCode = Left(LTrim(txtTelNum.Text) + "XXXXX", 5)
    'Other error checking is needed to remove spaces
    'and non-numeric characters

    Select Case DialCode

        Case "001" To "00199"
            lblCallType.Caption = "USA/Canada"

        Case "002" To "00999"
            lblCallType.Caption = "International (not USA/Can)"

        Case "01584", "01432", "60000" To "79999"
            lblCallType.Caption = "Local"

        Case "01100" To "09999"
            lblCallType.Caption = "National"

        Case "100" To "199XX"
            If Right(DialCode, 2) = "XX" Then
                lblCallType.Caption = "Operator service"
            Else
                lblCallType.Caption = "Invalid number"
            End If

        Case "999XX"
            lblCallType.Caption = "Emergency"

        Case Else
            lblCallType.Caption = "Invalid number"

    End Select

End Sub
```

Loops

The conditional statements give you the opportunity to decide whether or not some piece of code is to be executed but this still restricts you to a linear flow down through a procedure, from top to bottom. There are occasions when you also need to repeat a set of statements. Visual Basic provides looping instructions for every occasion:

- Repeating a section of code a number of times

- Repeating while a condition is true

- Repeating until a condition becomes true

- Repeating indefinitely

Each of these alternatives has its own set of Visual Basic instructions.

For...Next loops

The simplest approach to looping is to repeat a group of statements a given number of times. This is achieved with the **For...Next** statements, which have the following structure:

```
For variable = start To end Step step
    statements
Next variable
```

The loop begins with the *variable* set to the *start* value and the *statements* are executed. When the Next statement is reached the variable is increased by the *step* amount. If this is greater than the *end* value, the loop ends and execution continues with the statement below Next. Otherwise, the *statements* are executed again. This continues until the *end* value is exceeded.

The Step can be omitted, in which case the *variable* increases by 1 each time. The *step* may also be negative, reducing the variable value each time: in this case, the *end* should be less than the *start*.

For example:

```
For Country = 1 To 15
    listCountries.AddItem  CountryName(Country)
Next Country
```

This loop is repeated 15 times, with each value of Country from 1 to 15. Each time, the corresponding string from the array of country names is added to the list box.

You can **nest** one loop within another. In the following example, a control array of text boxes is set up (with one box for each day of the month). An initial text box is added to the form, with the Index property set to 0. The procedure for the form's **Load event** places the extra controls on the form, using the controls' **Load method**. Each control is then positioned on the form. The inner loop is executed 31 times. (This loop does not check the weekday of the first of the month, so the program is accurate only for months that begin on a Monday! This shortcoming is corrected in the Exercises.)

Calendar					

January 2001

Monday					
Tuesday					
Wednesday					
Thursday					
Friday					
Saturday					
Sunday					

See overleaf for program

Take note

If the *end* value is less than the *start* value when the loop is first entered (for a positive *step*), the *statements* will never be executed. Similarly, if the *end* is greater than the *start* for a negative *step*, the loop is omitted.

Calendar – Jan 2001

```vb
Private Sub Form_Load()

    Dim DCol As Integer      'Column number
    Dim DRow As Integer      'Row number
    Dim i As Integer         'Counter

    'Hide original text box
    'This text box has an Index of 0 and is
    'used only as the template for the
    'other text boxes in the control array
    txtDiaryEntry(0).Visible = False

    For DCol = 0 To 5
        'One column for each week

        For DRow = 0 To 6
            'One row for each day of the week

            'Calculate day number
            i = (DCol * 7) + DRow + 1

            'Load text box and display at correct offset
            'Assumes month starts on Monday!
            Load txtDiaryEntry(i)
            txtDiaryEntry(i).Left = 1440 + 1560 * DCol
            txtDiaryEntry(i).Top = 1080 + 600 * DRow
            txtDiaryEntry(i).Visible = True

            If i >= 31 Then
                'Get out of loop
                DRow = 6
                DCol = 5
            End If

        Next DRow

    Next DCol

End Sub
```

The Load event for a form occurs when a form is loaded into memory (for example, by the Show method). The Load statement for a control is executed as part of the program and has the effect of adding a control to the array.

You can use the Exit For statement as a shortcut to get out of a loop early. However, to make your procedures easier to understand, you should try to devise them so that you leave the loop at the Next statement.

Do loops

The **Do...Loop** group of statements provides an alternative to For...Next loops, repeating the loop until some condition is either true or false. There are five varieties of this loop:

Do *statements* Loop	Repeats until an Exit Do statement is encountered or the user presses **[Ctrl-Break]**
Do While *condition* *statements* Loop	Repeats as long as the condition is true; loop is never executed if the condition is false initially
Do *statements* Loop While *condition*	Repeats as long as the condition is true; loop is always executed at least once
Do Until *condition* *statements* Loop	Repeats until the condition is true; loop is never executed if the condition is true initially
Do *statements* Loop Until *condition*	Repeats until the condition is true; loop is always executed at least once

Each of these is useful in particular circumstances. The most important decision is whether to place the While/Until part of the structure at the top or bottom of the loop; this depends on whether or not you want the loop to be executed at least once, regardless of the initial state of the condition.

Choose between Until and While depending on which makes the condition easier to understand. An Until statement can be converted into a While statement by putting Not in front of the condition: for example, While A > 0 is the same as Until Not A > 0 or Until A <= 0.

You can use Exit Do to jump out of any loop but, where possible, this statement should be avoided; it is neater to exit via the Loop statement. The program below demonstrates the use of these loops.

Address labels

```
Private Sub cmdProcessAddress_Click()

    'Takes a full address from a single-line text box and displays
    'it in a multi-line text box, splitting it at the commas
    'Takes account of address starting with a number
    'and a comma

    Dim FullAddress As String
    Dim NextLine As String
    Dim FollowingHouseNumber As Boolean
    Dim LineNumber As Integer
    Dim Address(10) As String

    Const Comma = ","
    CR = Chr(13) & Chr(10)          'CR/Line feed

    'Get full address from text box
    FullAddress = txtFullAddress.Text
    'Point to first line of address array
    LineNumber = 1
    'Initialise indicator
    FollowingHouseNumber = False
    'Find first comma in address
    CommaPos = InStr(FullAddress, Comma)

    'Loop as long as a comma has been found
    Do While CommaPos > 0

        NextLine = Left(FullAddress, CommaPos – 1)
        If FollowingHouseNumber Then
            'Add to first address line
            Address(1) = Address(1) & ", " & NextLine
            FollowingHouseNumber = False
        Else
            'Put into next address line
            Address(LineNumber)=Left(FullAddress, CommaPos–1)
        End If
```

Indent the statements between Do and Loop to make it easier to see where the loops start and end.

If there is no operator, the expression is calculated as either True (non-zero) or False.

```vb
        If LineNumber = 1 And Len(NextLine) < 5 And _
                            Val(NextLine) > 0 Then
            'First part of address is a house number
            'so next time round loop add rest of line 1
            'Stay on Line 1
            FollowingHouseNumber = True
        Else
            'Beyond house number so move to next line
            LineNumber = LineNumber + 1
        End If

        'Cut out text that has been dealt with
        FullAddress = LTrim(Mid(FullAddress, CommaPos + 1))

        'Find next comma
        CommaPos = InStr(FullAddress, Comma)

    Loop

    'Put rest of text in array
    Address(LineNumber) = FullAddress

    'Now build up text in multi-line box (txtAddressLabel)
    LineNumber = 1              'Reset pointer
    txtAddressLabel.Text = ""   'Clear multi-line box

    'Loop as long as there is something in the array
    'Add each new line to existing text, with CR/LF characters
    'to start next piece of text on new line
    Do Until Address(LineNumber) = ""
        txtAddressLabel.Text = txtAddressLabel.Text & _
                            Address(LineNumber) & CR
        LineNumber = LineNumber + 1
    Loop

End Sub
```

Exercises

1   Write a single procedure to add a given number of days, weeks, calendar months or years to a given date, returning the calculated date and its day of the week (as a number). Create a form that uses the procedure to display the results for entered numbers.

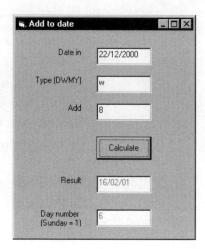

2   Write a function to check whether a password is valid. The function should return a value of True or False.

3   Write a program to display a calendar, as shown below. The display should be updated whenever the month or year is changed. The user should only be able to enter values in the blank cells to the right of the numbers.

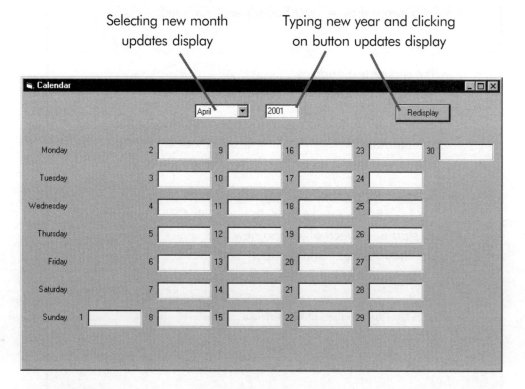

For solutions to these exercises, see page 182.

7 Error handling

Debugging

When the program encounters a problem it cannot handle, it displays an error message, giving you alternatives to end or **debug** the program.

If you click on the Debug button, the Code window is displayed with a box around the line that has caused the problem. The program has not halted; it has only been temporarily suspended. Therefore, if the error is not too serious, you can make a correction and continue running.

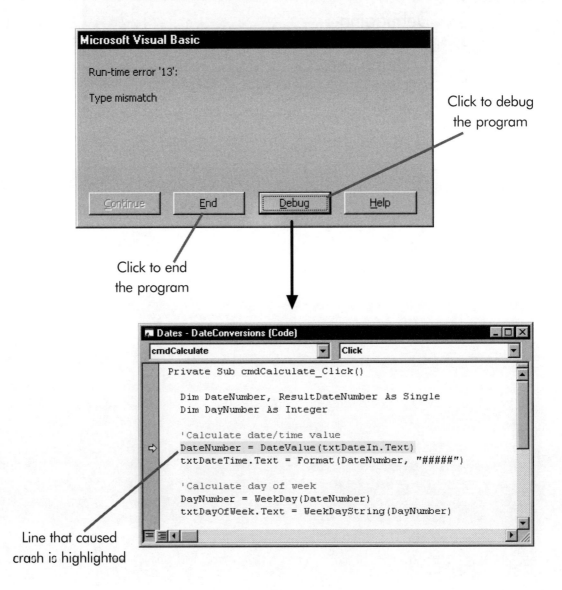

Click to debug
the program

Click to end
the program

Line that caused
crash is highlighted

Several options are available:

- You can change the line that caused the problem and then press **[F5]** (Run|Continue) to continue running the program.

- You can make more far-reaching changes to the program and then restart it by pressing **[Shift-F5]** (Run|Restart).

- You can close down the program by selecting Run|End.

- You can restart the program from a different point by clicking on another line, selecting Debug|Set Next Statement, and then pressing **[F5]** (Run|Continue). (This is not usually a successful option, as it may upset the logic of the program.)

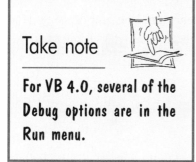

Take note

For VB 4.0, several of the Debug options are in the Run menu.

If you lose your place in the program, Debug|Show Next Statement displays the procedure containing the next statement to be executed.

While the program is halted, you can also inspect the values of variables or expressions (see *Watching variables* on page 125).

Sometimes the changes you make are such that Visual Basic cannot continue running the program. A warning message is displayed and, if you click on OK, the changes are accepted and the program must be restarted.

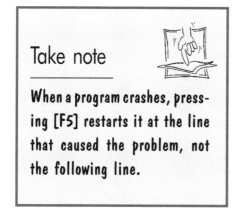

Take note

When a program crashes, pressing [F5] restarts it at the line that caused the problem, not the following line.

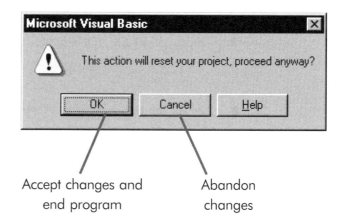

Accept changes and end program   Abandon changes

Breakpoints

You can force Visual Basic to halt execution at a particular point in the program by setting a **breakpoint**. Put the cursor on the required line and press **[F9]** (Debug|Toggle Breakpoint); alternatively, click on the grey area to the left of the line. The line is shown with a different-coloured background and a circle is displayed in the grey area. When the program is run, it will halt at this point, before the line is executed.

Having interrupted the program in this way, you can inspect the contents of variables, step through the code a line at a time, make minor changes to the code, or continue execution by pressing **[F5]**.

You can set several breakpoints at once; the program halts each time a breakpoint is encountered. A breakpoint can be cancelled by clicking on the breakpoint line and pressing **[F9]** again; all breakpoints can be cancelled with Debug|Clear All Breakpoints.

Take note

You can also break into a program by pressing [Ctrl-Break] or selecting Run|Break.

Single-stepping

When a program halts because of an error or a breakpoint, the line that is about to be executed is highlighted. You can now run the program a line at a time using the following options:

● Press **[F8]** (Debug|Step Into) to execute the line; if the line contains a procedure or a function call, the procedure or function is displayed and you can continue to step through it a line at a time. This is called **single-stepping**.

● Press **[Shift-F8]** (Debug|Step Over) to execute the line, including any procedure or function call; the next line in the current procedure is then highlighted.

● Move the cursor to some other point in the program and press **[Ctrl-F8]** (Debug|Run To Cursor); execution restarts and continues until this point is reached.

When you have finished single-stepping, you can use the Run options either to continue or to end the program.

Watching variables

Having broken into a program, you can inspect the values of any variables or expressions. If you put the cursor on a variable name in the code, the current value pops up below the name.

You can also see how the value changes as the program progresses. Click on a variable name or highlight an expression in the code; then select Debug|Add Watch. After confirming that this is the expression to watch, the Debug window is displayed. This shows the expression and its current value. Each time you use Add Watch, another expression is added to the Debug window. Now, as you single-step through the program, you will be able to see how the values of variables are affected by the code, making it much easier to identify the causes of problems.

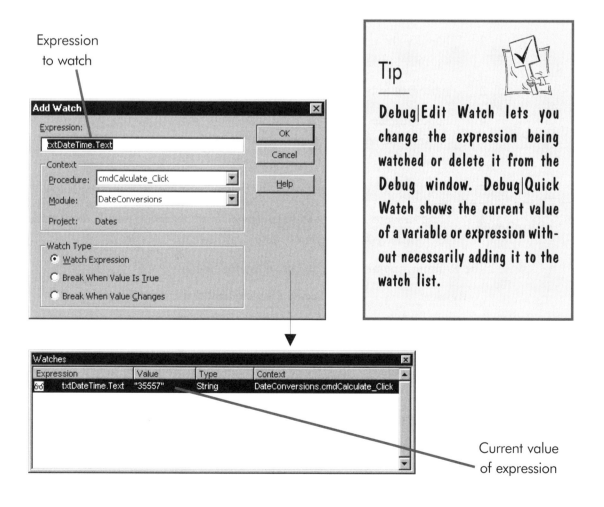

Expression to watch

Tip

Debug|Edit Watch lets you change the expression being watched or delete it from the Debug window. Debug|Quick Watch shows the current value of a variable or expression without necessarily adding it to the watch list.

Current value of expression

Trapping errors

You will have noticed that some of the programs you have been writing crash if an invalid entry is made (for instance, if a text box that is supposed to contain a date is blank when a button is clicked). You can test for some errors – and correct them – using a control's LostFocus event. To be sure of handling all errors, however, you should include error-trapping statements in your code. These statements are activated when an error occurs.

Error-trapping is implemented as follows:

1 Turn error-trapping on with a statement in the form:

On Error GoTo *label*

When a **trappable** error occurs (one that On Error GoTo can handle), the program jumps to the code pointed to by the *label*.

2 Identify the end of the normal part of the procedure with an Exit Sub statement (just above End Sub).

3 After Exit Sub, enter the *label*, adding a colon (:) to the end of it.

4 Following the *label*, insert the statements that will correct the error (for instance, statements to display a warning message or change the contents of a text box).

5 End the error-handling statements with a Resume statement (see below).

6 If the Resume statement includes a label, insert the label (with a colon) at the appropriate point in the procedure.

The **Resume** statement must be one of the following:

Resume	Re-execute the statement that caused the problem.
Resume Next	Continue with the statement following the one that caused the error.
Resume *label2*	Resume execution on the line following *label2*.

Most errors can be trapped, though only certain types of error are likely to occur in any procedure.

The procedure below demonstrates the use of error-trapping statements.

Error trapping

Sample procedure taken from Date Conversions program on pages 88-89.

```
Private Sub cmdCalculate_Click()

    'Amended to prevent program crashing
    'if an invalid date is entered (or the box is
    'blank) when the Calculate button is pressed

    Dim DateNumber As Single
    Dim ResultDateNumber As Single
    Dim DayNumber As Integer

    On Error GoTo BadDate
ErrorRestart:

    'Calculate date/time value
    DateNumber = DateValue(txtDateIn.Text)
    txtDateTime.Text = Format(DateNumber, "#####")

    'Calculate day of week
    DayNumber = WeekDay(DateNumber)
    txtDayOfWeek.Text = WeekDayString(DayNumber)

    'Calculate value for Result box
    ResultDateNumber = DateNumber + Val(txtAddDays.Text)
    txtResult.Text = Format(ResultDateNumber, "dd/mm/yyyy")

    'Update date/time label
    lblNow.Caption = "Date/time of last entry: " & Str(Now)

    Exit Sub

BadDate:

    'This routine is invoked if any error occurs but at
    'this stage handles only one type of error
    'Insert current date in box and then continue
    txtDateIn.Text = Date
    Resume ErrorRestart

End Sub
```

You can list the errors that On Error can handle by searching the on-line help for 'Trappable Errors'.

When an error occurs, the Err function returns the error number and Error holds the text of the error message.

Exercises

1   Use the debugging options to interrupt the Members program when the Region is changed; watch the text and label values as they are changed.

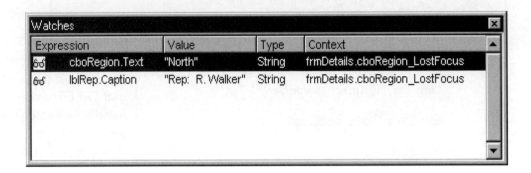

2   Add error-handling statements to the Calendar program so that it deals with a blank entry in the Year box.

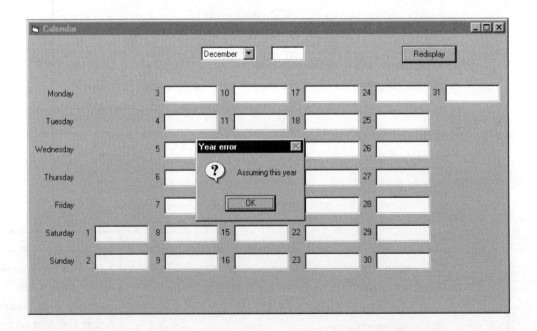

For solutions to these exercises, see page 186.

8 Menus

The Menu Editor

Properties for one menu item

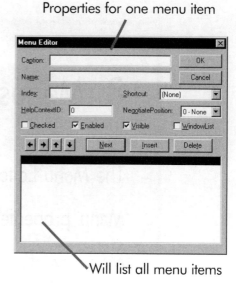

Drop-down menus are added to forms using the **Menu Editor**. Click on the form to which the menus are to be attached and select the Tools|Menu Editor option (or press **[Ctrl-E]**). The Menu Editor window is displayed. The upper half of the window shows the properties of an individual menu item; the lower half lists all the items in the menus for the current form.

Will list all menu items

Caption and Name

Each menu name and option name is a separate control and therefore has its own Caption and Name. The Caption is the word or phrase that will appear in the drop-down menu; include an & in front of the character that is to be used as an **access key** (e.g. &File for a menu that can be invoked by pressing **[Alt F]**). Traditionally, the Caption should end with three dots if the menu item leads to a dialog box.

The usual convention is for the Name to consist of 'mnu' followed by the sequence of options (e.g. mnuFileSave for a File|Save option).

Include & in front of access key

Adding options

When you have entered the first menu's Caption and Name, click on Next. The menu name is shown in the box in the lower half of the window and the highlighting moves to the next blank line.

The hierarchy of the menu structure is identified by levels of indent within the list of items. The items on the left of the window are the menu names that will appear in the menu bar. The options within a menu are listed below the menu

Menu options are indented below menu names

name and indented. If any option has a sub-menu, the sub-menu options are listed below with a further level of indent.

To add an option to the menu, click on the right-pointing arrow. Four dots appear, showing that this is an option in the menu above. The option can then be inserted.

When all the options have been entered for the menu, clicking on the left-pointing arrow removes the dots from the next line, allowing you to enter a new menu name.

Editing the menus

You can select an item by clicking on it. When an item is highlighted, you have the following options:

- Click on Insert to insert a new option above the current item.

- Click on Delete to remove the current item.

- Click on the left arrow to promote a menu option into a menu name.

- Click on the right arrow to change a menu name into an option for the menu above.

- Click on the up arrow to move an item up the list.

- Click on the down arrow to move an item down the list.

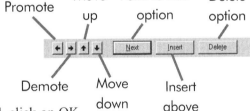

When all the items have been added, click on OK.

Sub-menus

As well as menus and options within menus, you can have sub-menus. These are created by adding options at a second level of indent, so that the first-level option effectively becomes a sub-menu name.

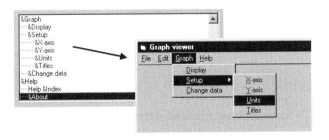

The sub-menu options can themselves become a further level of sub-menu by indenting the next set of items to a third level. In all, you can have up to four levels of sub-menus, though it is unusual to go beyond the first sub-menu.

Menu properties

Within the Menu Editor window there are a number of properties that can be set or changed for each menu item. The Caption and Name are described above; the other properties are detailed here.

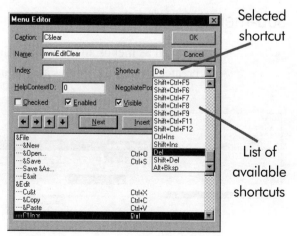

No tick next to option   Option can be selected   Option is visible

Boolean properties

The Menu Editor has check boxes for three Boolean properties:

- The **Checked** property, when set, places a tick on the left of the menu option.

- The **Enabled** property, when cleared, greys out the menu or option; clicking on the menu or option has no effect.

- The **Visible** property, when cleared, hides the option when the menu is displayed (or hides the menu).

Usually, you will want to leave the properties as they are when developing the menu system but change them while the program is running. For instance, an option may be used for switching some feature of the program on or off. Clicking on the option will set Enabled to True (and place a tick against it); clicking on it again will set Enabled to False (and remove the tick). As another example, after saving a file the File|Save option may have its Enabled property set to False; as soon as further changes are made to the data the Enabled property can be set to True again. The Visible property can be used for restricting options: for instance, some menu options may be visible only to users with certain passwords.

Shortcut keys

You can attach a **shortcut key** to any option in any of the menus. This is a key combination that the user can press to activate the menu option without having to click on the option itself. For example, it is usual for the File|Save option to have a

Selected shortcut

List of available shortcuts

[Ctrl-S] shortcut, so that the save routine is invoked when the user presses [Ctrl-S].

A shortcut is attached to an item by clicking on the shortcut box and then selecting from the drop-down list. When you run the program and display the menu, the shortcut is shown to the right of the option name.

All menu items should have an *access key* (a key used in combination with [Alt] to activate the option). Only the most frequently-used options should have *shortcuts* (which use keys other than [Alt]).

Separator bars

For long menus, its is useful to split the options into groups. This is done by inserting a separator bar. The bar is included as an item in the menu with a special caption of '–'. The separator bar must be given a Name (which will be needed if, for example, you want to make the bar invisible later).

Other properties

When you have created a menu system for a form, you can also alter each item's properties using the Properties window. Select the menu item from the drop-down list at the top of the window and then change the properties in the usual way.

Four other properties may be useful in more complex applications:

- **Index** holds an index number for arrays of menu items.

- **HelpContextID** provides a link to a help file.

- **NegotiatePosition** determines the position of a menu when some other object is also displaying a menu.

- **WindowList** determines whether or not the menu contains a list of other open windows.

Menu item properties

For more information on these properties, see the Visual Basic on-line *Language Reference*.

Menu events

Menu controls respond to a Click event, which is activated either by clicking on the menu option or by pressing the access key or shortcut.

For menus and sub-menus, the Click event results in the list of options dropping down. For menu options, you need to supply a Click procedure. The code for this is added in exactly the same way as for any other event. (You can either select the menu option name from the Object box or click on the option in the form's menu bar.)

Tip

Some menu options will duplicate the effect of other events. For instance, selecting the File|Exit option may be the same as clicking on the Exit button. In such cases, the menu option's Click event should call the procedure for the corresponding event (e.g. mnuFileExit_Click should call cmdExit_Click).

The Edit menu

Most applications have an Edit menu with the following options:

Cut   Deletes highlighted text and copies to clipboard

Copy   Copies highlighted text to clipboard

Paste   Pastes text from clipboard at cursor position (replacing any highlighted text)

Clear   Deletes highlighted text

The **clipboard** is an object that is supplied with every Windows application. It does not have any physical appearance or events but it does have some useful methods:

Clear   Clears the contents of the clipboard

SetText   Copies the specified text to the clipboard

GetText( )   Returns the contents of the clipboard

The clipboard methods can be used in conjunction with the following text box properties:

SelText   String of highlighted characters (blank if none selected)

SelLength   Length of highlighted string

SelStart   Current cursor position (0 if in front of first character)

The procedures below show how the Edit menu options are usually implemented.

Edit menu

```
Private Sub mnuEditCut_Click()
    'Assumes text being edited is in a text box called txtEntry
    Clipboard.Clear                    'Clear the clipboard
    Clipboard.SetText txtEntry.SelText 'Copy highlighted text
                                       'to clipboard

    txtEntry.SelText = ""              'Delete hightlighted text
End Sub

Private Sub mnuEditCopy_Click()
    Clipboard.Clear                    'Clear the clipboard
    Clipboard.SetText txtEntry.SelText 'Copy text to clipboard
End Sub

Private Sub mnuEditPaste_Click()
    'Replace highlighted text with contents
    'of clipboard
    txtEntry.SelText = Clipboard.GetText()
End Sub

Private Sub mnuEditClear_Click()
    'Clear the highlighted text
    'May want to add a warning message here
    txtEntry.Text = ""                 'Delete all text
End Sub
```

The GetText() method should be treated as a function rather than a procedure; i.e. it should be included on the right-hand side of an expression only.

Exercises

1   Add the following menu options to the Members program's main window:

Menu/option	Access key	Shortcut	Effect when clicked
File	f		(Menu)
Open...	o	Ctrl + O	(Leave empty)
Save...	s	Ctrl + S	(Leave empty)
Exit	x		Ends program
Window	w		(Menu)
Member Details...	m		Displays Details screen
Comments...	c		Displays Comments screen
Close All	a		Closes all other windows
Help			(Menu)
About	a		Displays information box

Create appropriate Click procedures for these options.

2   Add the following menu options to the Details window:

Menu/Option	Access key	Shortcut	Effect when clicked
File	f		(Menu)
Save...	s	Ctrl + S	(Leave empty)
Abandon	a		Same effect as Cancel
Exit	x		Same effect as OK

Create appropriate Click procedures for these options.

3   Add the following menu options to the Comments window:

Menu/Option	Access key	Shortcut	Effect when clicked
File	f		(Menu)
Save...	s	Ctrl + S	(Leave empty)
Abandon	a		Same effect as Cancel
Exit	x		Same effect as OK
Edit	e		(Menu)
Cut	t	Ctrl + X	Cuts text to clipboard
Copy	c	Ctrl + C	Copies text to clipboard
Paste	p	Ctrl + V	Paste text from clipboard
Clear	l		Deletes highlighted text (asks for confirmation)

Create appropriate Click procedures for these options.

For solutions to these exercises, see page 186.

9 Files

File selection

File list box

Directory box

Drive box

Visual Basic provides three standard controls to allow the user to select from lists of files, directories and drives. Each of these is a specialised type of list box.

- The **file list box** provides a simple list of files. The **Path** property holds the full directory path; the **Pattern** property restricts the list to those matching a file specification (e.g. *.bas); and the **FileName** property contains the currently-highlighted file. The file list box responds to **Click** and **DblClick** events.

- The **directory box** lists the directories for a drive. The **Path** property holds the full directory path (including drive). The directory box responds to **Click** and **Change** events.

- The **drive box** is a combo box that, when clicked, lists the available drives. The **Drive** property contains the selected drive. The drive box responds to the **Change** event.

The use of these controls is illustrated in the procedures below.

To make life easier, you can add a **Common Dialog** control to a form. This control provides standard Open, Save, Printer, Colour and Font dialog boxes, which are activated with the ShowOpen, ShowSave, ShowPrinter, ShowColor and ShowFont methods respectively.

To add the Common Dialog control to the toolbox, select Project|Components, click on the Microsoft Common Dialog Control check box and click on OK. The properties of the control vary depending on the type of dialog box selected. For example, to display an Open dialog box for bitmaps, add a Common Dialog control to a form, change its name to dlgOpen and invoke it with the following instructions:

```
Private Sub mnuFileOpen_Click()
    dlgOpen.Filter = "*.bmp"          'Restrict to bmp files
    dlgOpen.Filename = "*.bmp"        'Initial name to be displayed
    dlgOpen.ShowOpen                  'Display the box and get
                                      'the filename
            'dlgOpen.Filename now holds the selected filename
End Sub
```

A similar procedure can be used to invoke the Save dialog box from a File|Save As option.

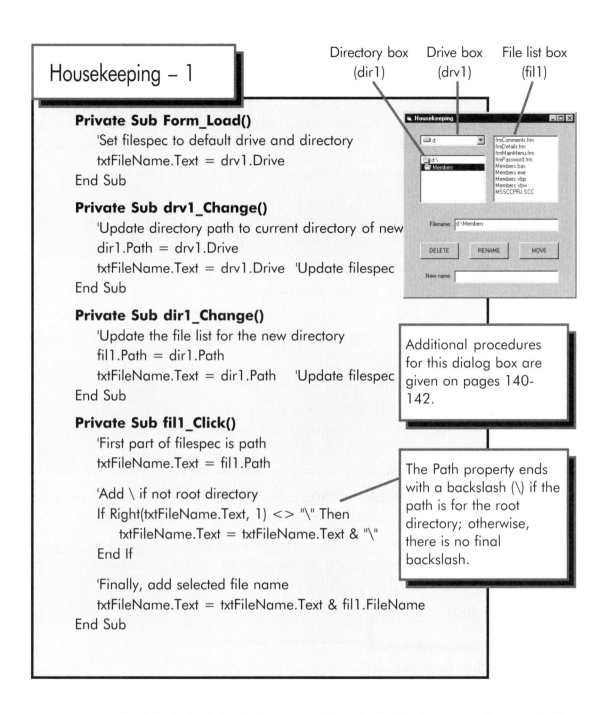

Housekeeping – 1

Directory box (dir1) Drive box (drv1) File list box (fil1)

```
Private Sub Form_Load()
    'Set filespec to default drive and directory
    txtFileName.Text = drv1.Drive
End Sub

Private Sub drv1_Change()
    'Update directory path to current directory of new
    dir1.Path = drv1.Drive
    txtFileName.Text = drv1.Drive   'Update filespec
End Sub

Private Sub dir1_Change()
    'Update the file list for the new directory
    fil1.Path = dir1.Path
    txtFileName.Text = dir1.Path     'Update filespec
End Sub

Private Sub fil1_Click()
    'First part of filespec is path
    txtFileName.Text = fil1.Path

    'Add \ if not root directory
    If Right(txtFileName.Text, 1) <> "\" Then
        txtFileName.Text = txtFileName.Text & "\"
    End If

    'Finally, add selected file name
    txtFileName.Text = txtFileName.Text & fil1.FileName
End Sub
```

Additional procedures for this dialog box are given on pages 140-142.

The Path property ends with a backslash (\) if the path is for the root directory; otherwise, there is no final backslash.

By default, the Drive is the current drive, the Path is the current directory for that drive, and the Pattern is *.* (i.e. all files).

You can further restrict the list in a file list box by setting the Archive, Hidden, ReadOnly and System properties. The Normal property identifies files for which none of these attributes is set.

File operations

Within a program, you may want to delete, rename or copy a file, or carry out directory operations. Visual Basic provides a means of handling all these tasks.

● The **Kill** statement deletes a file:

> Kill *filespec*

The *filespec* is a string containing the name of the file to be deleted. You can use the * and ? wildcards (e.g. *.TMP to delete all TMP files).

● The **Name** statement renames a file:

> Name *oldname* As *newname*

The *oldname* is a string containing the original path and name; *newname* is the file's new name. Only one file can be renamed at a time. If the new name contains a different path, the file will be moved to that directory.

● The **FileCopy** statement copies a file:

> FileCopy *source destination*

The *source* is a string containing the name of the file to be copied. The *destination* is the name of the new file. Both filenames may include the directory and drive if necessary. Only one file can be copied at a time.

● **MkDir**, **RmDir** and **ChDir** create, delete or change directories respectively. Each must be followed by a string containing the directory name.

The procedures below demonstrate the use of some of these instructions. They can be added to the Housekeeping dialog box above to provide a useful utility program.

Housekeeping – 2

The dialog box illustrated on page 139 uses these procedures.

```
Public Sub RedrawList()
    Dim CurrentPath As String

    'Change path and then change it back again to force redraw
    CurrentPath = fil1.Path
    fil1.Path = "c:\"
    fil1.Path = "c:\windows"  'In case c:\ already current directory
    fil1.Path = CurrentPath
```

```vb
    'Redo entry boxes
    fil1_Click                    'Recalculate filename
    txtNewName.Text = ""          'Clear new name
End Sub

Private Sub cmdDelete_Click()
    'Delete a file
    Dim Response As Integer
    On Error GoTo BadFile

    'Display warning message and get response
    Response = MsgBox("Delete " & txtFileName.Text, 308, _
                                    "Delete File")

    If Response = 6 Then
        Kill txtFileName.Text
    End If
    RedrawList                    'Update display
ExitProc:
    Exit Sub

BadFile:
    'Cannot delete (probably because open)
    MsgBox "Filename " & txtFileName.Text & _
                    " cannot be deleted", 16, "Delete File"
    Resume ExitProc               'Exit procedure
End Sub

Private Sub cmdRename_Click()
    Dim NewName As String
    'Rename a file
    On Error GoTo BadName

    'First part of new filename is path
    NewName = fil1.Path
    'Add \ if not root directory
    If Right(NewName, 1) <> "\" Then
        NewName = NewName & "\"
    End If
```

```vb
        'Finally, add entered file name
        NewName = NewName & txtNewName.Text
        Name txtFileName.Text As NewName
        RedrawList                 'Update display
        Exit Sub

BadName:
    'New filename is invalid
    MsgBox "Filename " & txtNewName.Text & " is invalid", _
                                    16, "Rename File"
    Resume Next                 'Resume at RedrawList
End Sub

Private Sub cmdMove_Click()
    Dim NewName As String
    'Rename a file
    On Error GoTo BadName

    'First part of new filename is path entered in New Name box
    NewName = txtNewName.Text
    'Add \ if not root directory
    If Right(NewName, 1) <> "\" Then
        NewName = NewName & "\"
    End If

    'Finally, add original file name
    NewName = NewName & fil1.filename
    Name txtFileName.Text As NewName
    RedrawList                 'Update display
    Exit Sub

BadName:
    'New path is invalid
    MsgBox "Path " & txtNewName.Text & " is invalid", 16, _
                                    "Rename File"
    Resume Next                 'Resume at RedrawList
End Sub
```

142

Sequential files

Sequential files consist of a series of lines of text, and are often referred to as **ASCII files**. Each line of text is terminated by a carriage-return character (ASCII 13) and the file ends with Ctrl-Z (ASCII 26). Although ASCII files can include extended ASCII characters, they are usually restricted to the standard characters, in the range 32 to 126. Sequential files are stored with one byte for each character and can be viewed, edited or created by Notepad or other text editors.

Visual Basic provides a group of instructions for handling sequential files. At their simplest, sequential files are written or read one complete line at a time (a line consisting of everything up to the next carriage-return character). Therefore, they are suitable for storing text: for example, the output from a multi-line text box.

Sequential files can also be saved in the **comma-delimited** format. In these files, each line consists of one or more data values, separated by commas. Text items should be enclosed in double quotes. When a line of data is read from a sequential file, each value is assigned to a variable.

Text file (ASCII file)

First joined December, 1997
Originally Associate
Became Full member January, 1999

Comma-delimited file

"Jim Smith", 1023, "Full", 20, "South"
"Jo Edwards", 1036, "Full", 20, "East"
"Ellen Howe", 1045, "Associate", 12, "South"

Take note

You cannot both read and write to a sequential file at the same time. Each time you open a file it is for either reading or writing.

Take note

Text in comma-delimited files does not have to be enclosed in quotes but it is less confusing if it is. If the text contains a comma, double quotes must be used around the item containing the comma, otherwise it will be treated as two separate items.

Creating sequential files

There are three stages in creating a sequential file: opening the file, writing the data and closing the file. The file is **opened** with a statement in the form:

Open *filename* For *mode* As *#number*

If the *mode* is 'Output', a new file is created and any existing file with the same name is deleted. If the *mode* is 'Append', the new data is added to the end of the existing file (or a new file is created, if one does not yet exist).

The *number* identifies the file in the rest of the program and must be in the range 1 to 255. The number is linked to the file only as long as the file is open. When the file is closed, the number can be re-used for another file; if a file is re-opened it does not have to be assigned the same number as before.

Data is written to a sequential file with the **Print** or **Write** statements. Each statement writes one line of data to the file, terminated by a carriage return. The format of these statements is as follows:

Print *#number, value1, value2, ...*
Write *#number, value1, value2, ...*

The Print statement writes data with tabs between separate items; this statement is suitable for writing text files (with just one item per line). The Write statement stores data in comma-delimited format.

The file is **closed** with a statement in the form:

Close *#number*

The Close statement is essential, as it stores away any unwritten data held in memory.

Take note

You can also create binary files, where data is written and read a character at a time. This gives you complete control over the file, without having to worry about the structure imposed by comma-delimited files or record-based files. However, your program must keep precise track of the position and size of data in the file.

Reading sequential files

Corresponding to the creation of a sequential file, there are three stages for reading such a file: opening the file, reading the data and closing the file.

The file is **opened** with the following statement:

Open *filename* For Input As *#number*

Data is read from the file with one of these statements:

Line Input *#number, string*

Input *#number, variable1, variable2, ...*

The **Line Input** statement reads an entire line into a *string* and is suitable for text files. The Input statement should be used where files have been written with the Write statement.

The **Close** statement is the same as before.

Sequential files are always read from the beginning of the file. You can use the **EOF** function to detect the end of the file. (The function returns a True value when the end-of-file marker has been reached.) The **LOF** function gives you the length of the file (in bytes) and **LOC** returns the current location (in terms of the number of characters read so far). All three functions take the file number as their argument.

The following procedures demonstrate how File|Open and File|Save commands can be created to read and write data entered in the Calendar program created in the Chapter 6 Exercises. The File|Save procedure stores the contents of the calendar boxes in a sequential file, with one line for each box. The filename is based on the year and month of the calendar. The File|Open procedure reads the text back into the boxes.

Take note

Although the Input statement usually reads a complete line of data, it does not have to read all the values in a line at once and may continue from the end of one line onto the next. Alternatively, you may use several Input statements to read successive parts of a single line in the file.

Additions to Calendar program from page 120.

```
Private Sub mnuFileOpen_Click()

    'Loads calendar data when user presses [Ctrl-O]
    'Should also be called at end of ViewCalendar procedure so
    'that data automatically loads when user chooses new month

    Dim CalFile As String, CalSpec As String
    Dim i As Integer, DayNo As Integer
    Dim DiaryEntry As String

    On Error GoTo FileError
    Const CalDir = "c:\calendar\"          'Assume directory
                                           'already exists
    'Construct filename for storing calendar contents
    'Assumes boxes are called cboMonth and txtYear
    CalFile = Left(cboMonth.Text, 3) & txtYear.Text
    CalSpec = CalDir & CalFile & ".txt"

    'Read entries until end-of-file reached
    Open CalSpec For Input As #1
    Do While Not EOF(1)
        Input #1, i, DayNo, DiaryEntry
        txtDiaryEntry(i).Text = DiaryEntry
    Loop
    Close #1

ExitProc:
    Exit Sub

FileError:
    'Cannot open (probably because no file or no directory)
    If Err <> 53 Then
        'Don't display this message if error is File Not Found
        MsgBox "Cannot open file " & CalSpec, 16, "Open File"
    End If
    Resume ExitProc                        'Exit procedure
End Sub
```

```
Private Sub mnuFileSave_Click()

    'Saves when user presses [Ctrl-S]
    'Should also be called by txtDiaryEntry_LostFocus
    'so that file is updated each time an entry is made

    Dim CalFile As String
    Dim CalSpec As String
    Dim i As Integer
    Dim DayNo As Integer

    'On Error GoTo FileError
    Const CalDir = "c:\calendar\"          'Assume directory
                                           'already exists
    'Construct filename for storing calendar contents
    CalFile = Left(cboMonth.Text, 3) & txtYear.Text
    CalSpec = CalDir & CalFile & ".txt"

    'Write away entries if not blank
    Open CalSpec For Output As #2
    For i = 1 To 37        'Max number of boxes that can be used
        If txtDiaryEntry(i).Text > "" Then   'An entry has been made
            DayNo = Val(lblDayNo(i).Caption)   'Get date
            'Write text box number, day number and text
            Write #2, i, DayNo, txtDiaryEntry(i).Text
        End If
    Next i
    Close #2

ExitProc:
    Exit Sub

FileError:
    'Cannot save (probably because no directory)
    MsgBox "Cannot save file " & CalSpec, 16, "Save File"
    Resume ExitProc                 'Exit procedure
End Sub
```

You can check the contents of the file using Notepad.

Random access files

Random access files store data in a record-based format. The file consists of a number of records, each of which has the same size and layout. The advantage over sequential files is that you can read and write records in any order; records are accessed by specifying a record number. However, random access files are not suitable for variable-length data.

Record structure

You must define the structure of the records before attempting to read or write them. This is done with a **Type** declaration, which has the following form:

```
Type recordtype
    variable1 As type
    variable2 As type
    ...
End Type
```

Any string variables must be given an explicit length by declaring them as follows:

```
variable As String * length
```

For example:

```
CompanyName As String * 40      'Name can be up to 40 chars.
```

The Type statement is usually included in the (Declarations) section of the form or module.

Accessing records

Records are read or written in three stages: opening the file; reading or writing the data; and closing the file.

The **Open** statement has the following format:

```
Open filename For Random As #number Len = length
```

The Len part of the statement gives the record length; if omitted, the length defaults to 128 bytes. The sizes of different types of variables are given on page 76. You can also use the Len function to calculate the total length of the record.

Once opened, you can both write to and read from the file; you do not need to close the file in between the writing and reading operations.

To write records, you must first declare a variable of the record type previously defined. This will be in the format:

Dim *record* As *recordtype*

You must then fill the record by assigning values to the individual variables, using statements in the format:

recordtype.variable = *expression*

A completed record is written with a **Put** statement, as follows:

Put *#number, recordnumber, recordtype*

The *recordnumber* starts at 1 for the first record. If the number is beyond the current end-of-file, the file is extended. (Unused records will contain rubbish unless specifically cleared.)

Data is read from the file using a **Get** statement, as follows:

Get *#number, recordnumber, recordtype*

The individual variables in the *recordtype* are filled with the corresponding data from the record.

The procedures below provide alternative File operations for the Calendar program, this time storing the data in a random access file.

Take note

The EOF, LOC and LOF functions can be used with random access files. EOF is of little use, since you are not usually reading a file from beginning to end. LOF gives the length of the file in bytes. LOC returns the number of the last record read or written.

Tip

You can calculate the number of records in a random access file by dividing LOF by the record length. To get the record length, use LEN with the record variable as its argument.

Calendar files – 2

Additions to Calendar program from page 120 (see also page 146).

(Declarations) (Form)
```
Private Type CalendarType
    DayNumber As Integer
    TextEntry As String * 30     'Max 30 characters per box
End Type

Private Sub mnuFileOpen_Click()
    Dim CalFile As String, CalSpec As String
    Dim i As Integer, DayNo As Integer
    Dim DiaryEntry As String
    Dim RecLen As Integer
    Dim CalendarRec As CalendarType 'Declare record variable

    On Error GoTo FileError
    Const CalDir = "c:\calendar\"   'Assume directory exists
    'Construct filename for storing calendar contents
    CalFile = Left(cboMonth.Text, 3) & txtYear.Text
    CalSpec = CalDir & CalFile & ".dat"
    RecLen = Len(CalendarRec)
    Open CalSpec For Random As #1 Len = RecLen
    If LOF(1) > 0 Then        'Read entries if file previously saved
        For i = 1 To 37
            Get #1, i, CalendarRec              'Read record
            txtDiaryEntry(i).Text = Trim(CalendarRec.TextEntry)
        Next i
    End If
    Close #1
ExitProc:
    Exit Sub

FileError: 'Cannot open (probably no file or no directory)
    If Err <> 53 Then
        'Don't display this message if error is File Not Found
        MsgBox "Cannot open file " & CalSpec, 16, "Open File"
    End If
    Resume ExitProc                 'Exit procedure
End Sub
```

```
Private Sub mnuFileSave_Click()

    Dim CalFile As String, CalSpec As String
    Dim i As Integer, DayNo As Integer
    Dim RecLen As Integer
    Dim CalendarRec As CalendarType   'Declare record variable

    On Error GoTo FileError

    Const CalDir = "c:\calendar\"   'Assume directory exists

    'Construct filename for storing calendar contents
    'Assumes boxes are called cboMonth and txtYear
    CalFile = Left(cboMonth.Text, 3) & txtYear.Text
    CalSpec = CalDir & CalFile & ".dat"

    RecLen = Len(CalendarRec)
    Open CalSpec For Random As #2 Len = RecLen

    'Write away entries if not blank
    For i = 1 To 37      'Max number of boxes that can be used
        DayNo = Val(lblDayNo(i).Caption)     'Get date
                                             'Set up record:
        CalendarRec.DayNumber = DayNo            ' Field 1
        CalendarRec.TextEntry = txtDiaryEntry(i).Text ' Field 2
        Put #2, i, CalendarRec                'Write record
    Next i
    Close #2

ExitProc:
    Exit Sub

FileError:
    'Cannot save (probably because no directory)
    '(Can be expanded to deal with specific errors)
    MsgBox "Cannot save file " & CalSpec, 16, "Save File"
    Resume ExitProc                       'Exit procedure

End Sub
```

Exercises

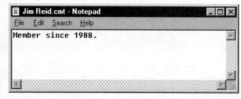

1 In the Membership program, add a combo box to the Main Menu to hold a list of members. Allow new names to be typed at the top of the Combo box. Add a command button which, when clicked, will add any new name to the list in the combo box.

2 Add code to the File|Save As option to create a file with a MEM extension (using a standard dialog box to enter the name). The file should contain the list of members.

3 Add code for File|Save to update the membership file and for File|Open to fill the combo box from the list in the file.

4 Add code for the File|Save option on the Comments screen. The current comments should be added to a text file with a filename based on the member's name. The OK button should also save the comments.

5 Add code so that the current member's comments (if any) are displayed when the Comments screen is loaded.

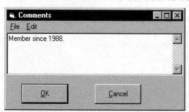

6 Add code for the File|Save option on the Details screen. The member's details should be stored as a single record in a file with the same name as the membership list file but an extension of DTL. The OK button should also save the data.

7 Add code so that the current member's details (if any) are displayed when the Details screen is loaded.

For solutions to these exercises, see page 188.

152

10 Graphics

Pictures

Image

PictureBox

The **picture box** control displays a bitmap file, icon file or metafile. (These have extensions of BMP, ICO and WMF respectively.) The **image** control is similar to the picture box but has fewer properties and methods. However, images are drawn faster than pictures.

The **Picture** property can be set at design time and specifies the filename of the picture to be displayed. In that case, the picture file is incorporated into the form file (and hence in the executable file, making it considerably larger). Alternatively, you can specify the filename at run time with the **LoadPicture** function; the picture file is then held separately from the executable file (but must be supplied with the application).

The **Height** and **Width** properties set the size of the picture box; if the box is not large enough for the whole picture, the top left-hand corner of the picture is displayed. For picture boxes, the box expands to fit the picture if **AutoSize** is True. The image control has a **Stretch** property, which, if set to True, results in the image being stretched to fit the box.

The **Left** and **Top** properties determine the position of the picture on the form. The **Move** method moves the picture to a new position.

The **Visible** property can be set to False to hide the picture. Therefore, using one or more pictures, you can create simple animations, as demonstrated by the procedure below.

```
Private Sub Form_Click()              'Starts when form is clicked
    Dim horiz As Integer, vert As Integer
    horiz = 1         'Horizontal direction; start going right
    vert = 1          'Vertical direction; start going down
    Do                'Continues until [Ctrl-Break] pressed
        img1.Move img1.Left + horiz * 10, img1.Top + vert * 10
        If img1.Left + img1.Width >= Form1.ScaleWidth Then _
                                              horiz = -1
        If img1.Left <= 0 Then horiz = 1
        If img1.Top + img1.Height >= Form1.ScaleHeight Then _
                                              vert = -1
        If img1.Top <= 0 Then vert = 1
    Loop
End Sub
```

Lines and shapes

The **line** control draws a line; **shape** adds a rectangle or oval.

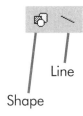

Line

Shape

The start of the line is given by the **X1** and **Y1** properties, the end by **X2** and **Y2.** These properties use the same co-ordinate system (in twips) as for other controls. X1 and X2 give the distance from the left of the form; Y1 and Y2 specify the position relative to the top. The appearance of the line is determined by **BorderColor**, **BorderStyle** and **BorderWidth**.

The shape control has a **Shape** property, which determines the type of shape, as follows:

0	Rectangle	**3**	Circle
1	Square	**4**	Rounded rectangle
2	Ellipse	**5**	Rounded square

The position and size of the shape are set by **Left**, **Top**, **Width** and **Height**. The **BorderColor**, **BorderStyle** and **BorderWidth** properties determine the appearance of the line around the edge of the shape; the inside colour and pattern are set by **FillColor** and **FillStyle**.

The program below demonstrates the use of these shapes, with colour and animation.

Name: shpSun
Shape: 3 – Circle
FillStyle: 0 – Solid
FillColor: Black
BorderStyle: Transparent
Left, Top: 3000, 3480
Width x Height: 615 x 495

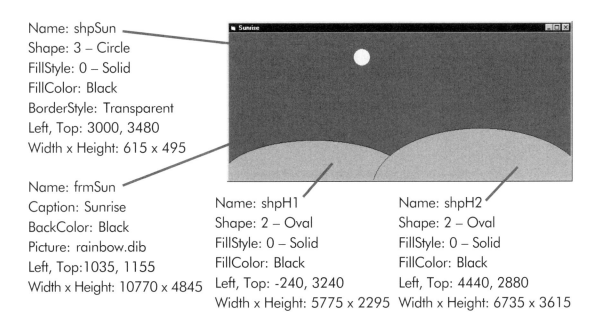

Name: frmSun
Caption: Sunrise
BackColor: Black
Picture: rainbow.dib
Left, Top:1035, 1155
Width x Height: 10770 x 4845

Name: shpH1
Shape: 2 – Oval
FillStyle: 0 – Solid
FillColor: Black
Left, Top: -240, 3240
Width x Height: 5775 x 2295

Name: shpH2
Shape: 2 – Oval
FillStyle: 0 – Solid
FillColor: Black
Left, Top: 4440, 2880
Width x Height: 6735 x 3615

```
Private Sub Form_Click()

    Dim Wid As Integer
    Dim Ht As Integer
    Dim IncrNo As Integer
    Dim i As Integer
    Dim j As Long
    Dim MoveIncr As Single
    Dim ColIncrNo As Integer
    Dim ColIncr As Integer

    Const Pi = 3.14159
    Const SpeedControl = 300000      'Increase to make slower
    Const Incr = 10                  'No. twips per move
    Const ColStages = 100            'No. times to change colour
    'Increasing value of ColStages gives more colour gradation
    'but more flicker

    'Hide sun until needed to reduce flicker
    shpSun.Visible = False

    Wid = frmSun.Width               'Form width
    Ht = frmSun.Height               'Form height
    IncrNo = Wid / Incr              'No. increments across screen
    ColIncrNo = Int(IncrNo / ColStages)
                                     'No. loops before colour changes

    For i = 0 To IncrNo              'Main loop

        'Calculate increment using sine wave
        MoveIncr = Sin((i / IncrNo) * Pi)
        ColIncr = Int(256 * MoveIncr)  'Colour increment

        'Set colours every ColIncrNo times through the loop
        If i / ColIncrNo = i \ ColIncrNo Then
            'Increment blue & green
            frmSun.BackColor = RGB(0, ColIncr / 2, ColIncr)
            shpH1.FillColor = RGB(0, ColIncr, ColIncr / 4)
```

```
                    shpH2.FillColor = RGB(0, ColIncr, 0)
                End If

                shpSun.Left = i * Incr
                shpSun.Top = Ht – Ht * MoveIncr

                If i < IncrNo / 2 Then                'First half
                    If shpSun.Top < shpH1.Top Then
                        shpSun.Visible = True
                    End If
                Else                                  'Second half
                    frmSun.Caption = "Sunset"
                    If shpSun.Top > shpH1.Top + 100 Then
                        shpSun.Visible = False        'Reduce flicker
                    End If
                End If

                For j = 1 To SpeedControl: Next j     'Delay

            Next i

            Unload frmSun                             'Close down

        End Sub
```

The program uses three shapes on the form. Two of the shapes are fixed, the third moves across the screen as a counter is incremented. Meanwhile, the colours of the two fixed shapes and the form background are varied with each increment.

The procedure shows that colour and shape can be used to enhance a program, although Visual Basic is not suitable for sophisticated graphics programs.

Form and picture box methods

You can also draw on the surface of forms and picture boxes using their **Line** and **Circle** methods. Any existing graphics can be cleared using the **Cls** method.

The **Print** method 'prints' text directly on the form or picture box. The font is changed with the **Font** property.

157

Printing

The contents of a form can be printed to the standard Windows printer using the **PrintForm** method.

For example, the following procedure can be added to the Calendar program to print the calendar for a month.

```
Private Sub mnuFilePrint_Click()
    frmCalendar.PrintForm
End Sub
```

This will print an exact copy of the form as currently displayed.

Printer commands

The **Printer** object is used for giving commands directly to the printer. Using this object, you can set up a page with individual pieces of text and images and then instruct Windows to print the finished page.

The object's **Print** method adds a specific piece of text to the output (but does not actually print anything). The text is added at the current printing position, using the current font.

The Printer object has a number of properties that affect the way in which each item of text is printed. The position on the page is set by the **CurrentX** and **CurrentY** properties. The various **Font** properties determine the appearance of the text.

Two other useful methods for the Printer object are **NewPage**, which starts a new page, and **EndDoc**, which tells Windows that the page has been set up.

The following program demonstrates the use of these commands.

Tip

You should always end a set of printer commands with an EndDoc instruction, so that Windows knows that the data is ready to be sent to the printer.

Take note

The PrintForm method automatically sends an EndDoc command when the form is ready to be printed.

Report printing

```vb
Private Sub mnuFilePrint_Click()

    Dim TitleMsg As String
    Dim TitleWidth As Integer

    On Error GoTo PrinterError

    TitleMsg = "Annual Report"              'Prepare title
    Printer.Font.Bold = True
    Printer.Font.Size = 24
    TitleWidth = Printer.TextWidth(TitleMsg)
    'Centre horizontally on paper, then print title
    Printer.CurrentX = (Printer.ScaleWidth – TitleWidth) / 2
    Printer.CurrentY = 1000
    Printer.Print TitleMsg
    Printer.Font.Bold = False
    Printer.Font.Size = 10
    Printer.CurrentX = Printer.ScaleWidth – 2000
    Printer.CurrentY = Printer.ScaleHeight – 2000
    Printer.Print "Page " & Printer.Page    'Print page no.
    Printer.NewPage                         'Form feed

    PrintContents          'Call procedure to print contents page
    Printer.CurrentX = Printer.ScaleWidth – 2000
    Printer.CurrentY = Printer.ScaleHeight – 2000
    Printer.Print "Page " & Printer.Page
    Printer.EndDoc                          'Send to printer

    frmMonthlyDetails.PrintForm             'Print second page
    frmSummary.PrintForm                    'Print final page
    Exit Sub

PrinterError:
    MsgBox "Cannot print the document", 16, "Print Report"
    Resume Next

End Sub
```

Exercises

1   Add a bitmap to the Members program's main menu.

2   Add a File|Print command to the Members program's Main Menu window, so that the full details, including comments, can be printed.

For solutions to these exercises, see page 193.

11 External databases

Accessing databases

Many applications are completely self-contained, creating and storing their own data and having no direct connection to other applications. However, most organisations have large amounts of information stored in a variety of database formats and some of your applications will need access to this data. Visual Basic includes a range of facilities for linking to external databases, allowing you to read and update their data. This section gives some simple examples to demonstrate Visual Basic's capabilities.

Take note

Some of the features described in this chapter are only available in the Professional and Enterprise editions.

Database elements

In order to access an external database, Visual Basic needs the following elements:

Data source control
(creates database and
recordset objects)

Data-aware control
(database grid)

- A **database** object. This defines the external database and allows your program to connect to the database and run queries on the data.

- A **recordset** object. This represents the records in the database (or the results of a query) and is used for viewing or editing the data.

- One or more **data-aware controls**. These display the contents of the database and allow users to make changes to the data.

- A **data source** control. This provides the link between the recordset and the data-aware controls.

For simple access to a database, you need be concerned only with the data source and data-aware controls; the rest is handled for you.

Database and recordset objects

The database and recordset objects provide the link between Visual Basic and the external database. The objects are not visible on the form; they are merely the means of defining and acessing the database.

These objects are created for you, using the properties of the data source control, when the form containing the control is created (but before the form's Load event is executed). Therefore, you do not have to create these objects (though there are instructions available should you need to do so). However, you can use the objects' methods and properties in your code. For example, if you have a data source control named Data1, you can select the first record of the recordset with the instruction:

    Data1.RecordSet.MoveFirst

Similar instructions are used for the database object.

Adding controls

The following example shows how to view and edit data from a sample Access file supplied with Visual Basic 6.0. The file contains lists of books and authors. In order to set up the application you need to add two controls to the toolbox:

1   Select Project|Components.

2   Select the Microsoft ADO Data Control and Microsoft DataGrid Control.

3   Click on OK.

The new controls are added to the toolbox. These controls will appear on the toolbox only when this particular application is open.

Click to add controls to toolbox

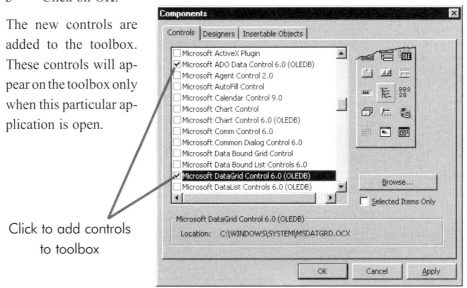

Data sources

The first stage in setting up the application is to add a data source, which tells the data-aware controls where to get their data:

1 Add an **ADO Data** control from the toolbox. As well as linking the form to the physical database, this control also provides a navigator bar for moving through the records. Resize the control (the caption in the middle does not have to be visible).

2 Change the control's Name (e.g. datBooks).

3 You must prepare the control for creating the database and recordset objects.

Double-click on the control's ConnectionString property so that the Property Pages dialog is displayed. Click on Build.

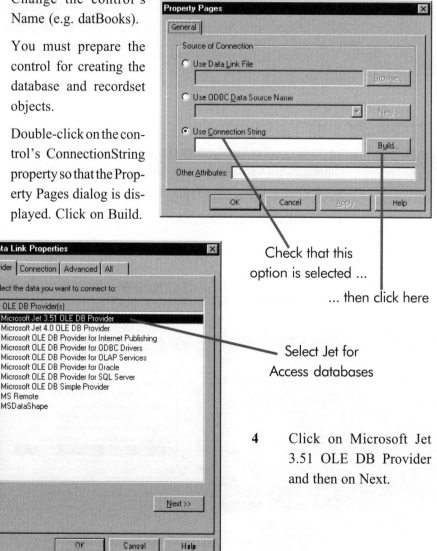

Check that this option is selected ...

... then click here

Select Jet for Access databases

4 Click on Microsoft Jet 3.51 OLE DB Provider and then on Next.

5   In the Connection page, click on the [...] button to the right of the first text box and select Biblio.mdb from the Visual Basic directory.

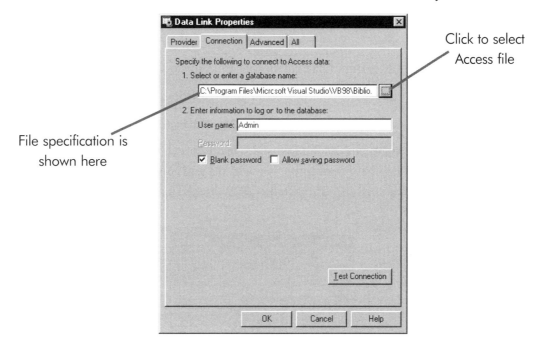

Click to select Access file

File specification is shown here

6   Click on Test Connection to check that everything is set up correctly, then close all the dialogs.

7   Double-click on the RecordSource property. Change the Command Type to cmdTable and select Authors as the Table. Click on OK.

You how have a visible data source control, which will create both a database object to connect the form to the Biblio.mdb Access database and a recordset object to connect to the Authors table within that database.

Take note

You can change the **ConnectionString** and **RecordSource** settings while the program is running, so that the form can display other tables or open a different database.

Data-aware controls

The second stage is to add controls for displaying and updating the data. This is useful if you want to build up a form that displays a single record.

In the current example, the whole file will be displayed on the form, so a grid control is needed:

1   Add a **Data Grid** component from the toolbox and resize it.

2   Change the control's Name (e.g. grdBooks).

3   Set the DataSource property (e.g. datBooks).

4   Right-click on the grid and select Retrieve Fields. If all the definitions and links have been correctly made, the grid columns are labelled appropriately. Initially, the grid includes all the fields but no data.

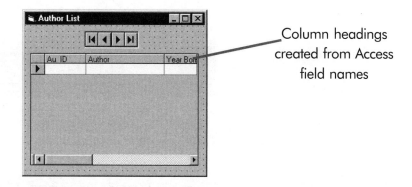

Column headings created from Access field names

5   In order to reduce the number of fields shown, right-click and select Edit. You can now change the column widths or alter the fields displayed. Right-clicking again gives you menu options to delete, insert or append columns; the Properties option lets you change other aspects of the grid, such as the colour and font, or the contents of each column.

6   Add statements in the code for the form's Resize procedure to make the grid expand to fit the form. For example:

```
grdBooks.Left = 0
grdBooks.Width = frmBooks.ScaleWidth
grdBooks.Height = frmBooks.ScaleHeight - grdBooks.Top
```

The form now contains everything you need for users to access the database.

166

Running the application

Press **[F5]** to run the application. The display shows the database grid. The window can be resized and the scroll bars and navigator buttons can be used to move around the data. The existing records can be edited. (Each changed record is stored away automatically when you move to another row on the grid or close the program.) The result is an effective database-access program, which has required only three lines of code.

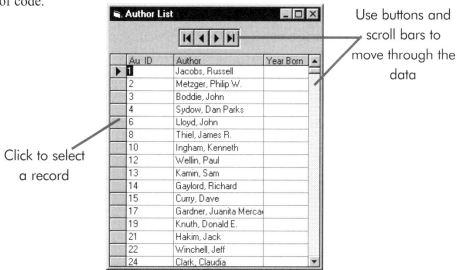

Use buttons and scroll bars to move through the data

Click to select a record

If you want to be able to insert or delete records, set the grid's AllowAddNew and AllowDelete properties to True. (Note that, in this example, the Author ID for new records is inserted for you when the database is saved.)

Using the data

You can access the data using the recordset's GetRows method, which has three parameters:

- The number of rows to retrieve

- The first row to be retrieved

- The field number (starting at 0 for the first field)

If you omit the last two parameters, the whole record is retrieved.

The retrieved data is stored in a two-dimensional variant array, where the first dimension specifies the field (0 for the first field retrieved) and the second contains the data.

For example, the second field (Author) for the currently selected row can be put into a text box with the following statements:

```
Dim Authors As Variant
Authors = datBooks.Recordset.GetRows(1, adBookmarkCurrent, 1)
Text1.Text = "Author: " & Authors(0, 0)
```

The GetRows method retrieves just one record in this case: the current record, identified by adBookmarkCurrent. The final parameter of 1 indicates that only the second field is required. The results of the method are stored in the variant array, which is dimensioned accordingly. The element Authors(0, 0) refers to the first (and only) field and the first (and only) item of data for that field.

The following statements place two full records into a pair of text boxes as follows:

```
Private Sub cmdSelect_Click()
    Dim Authors As Variant
    Authors = datBooks.Recordset.GetRows(2)
    Text1.Text = Authors(0, 0) & " : " & Authors(1, 0) & " : " _
                                          & Authors(2, 0)
    Text2.Text = Authors(0, 1) & " : " & Authors(1, 1) & " : " _
                                          & Authors(2, 1)

End Sub
```

Here, only one parameter has been given for the GetRows method, so the program assumes that the starting point for record retrieval is the current record and that all fields are to be retrieved.

The first element of the Authors array can now take the values 0, 1 or 2, representing the three fields of the table, while the second element can be either 0 or 1 to represent the two rows that have been retrieved.

This has demonstrated just a small number of Visual Basic's facilities for retrieving and updating data and running queries on databases of all types. For more information, see *ADO Overview* in the on-line help.

Internet access

As well as the data held on users' databases or networks, much information is available on the Internet. Many organisations have their own web sites, containing data that must be updated regularly. Using Visual Basic, you can set up sophisticated Internet applications that allow you to control and maintain your web sites.

Among the many facilities contained in Visual Basic for Internet communication, there is a **Web Browser** control for accessing existing web sites. This control can be added to the toolbox by selecting Project|Components and then choosing the Microsoft Internet Controls option. You do not have to make any changes to this control's properties for it to work (apart from cosmetic settings, such as size and position).

The Web Browser has some useful events (for example, **OnDocumentComplete**, which is invoked when a page has been downloaded). The control also has methods to execute all the usual browser actions. The **Navigate** method loads a web page, while **GoSearch** loads the search engine specified in the user's registry. **GoBack** takes you back to the last page in the history list. Similarly, **GoForward**, **GoHome**, **Stop** and **Refresh** mimic the effects of the buttons found on most web browsers. There are also some properties that are only available at run time: for example, **LocationURL**, which gives the address of the page currently being displayed.

The program over the page creates a simple web browser application. When the program is run, it connects to the Internet and loads the specified home page. The command buttons allow you to navigate around to other sites.

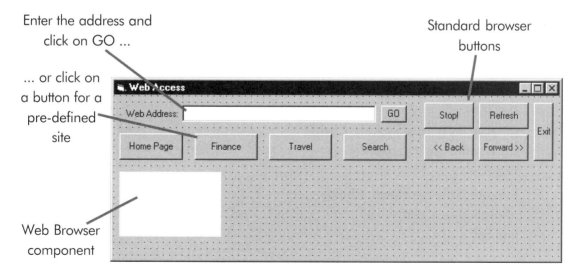

Enter the address and click on GO ...

... or click on a button for a pre-defined site

Web Browser component

Standard browser buttons

169

Internet addresses grouped at top of program to make future changes easy.

(Declarations)
Const HomePage = "www.netscapeonline.co.uk"
Const FinancePage = "ibank.barclays.co.uk"
Const TravelPage="212.87.65.227/bin/query.exe/enbin/query.exe/en"

Public Sub NavigateToPage(WebAddress As String)
    WebBrowser1.Navigate (WebAddress)
End Sub

Private Sub Form_Load()
    NavigateToPage (HomePage)
End Sub

Private Sub Form_Resize()
    WebBrowser1.Left = 0
    WebBrowser1.Width = WebForm.ScaleWidth
    WebBrowser1.Height=WebForm.ScaleHeight-WebBrowser1.Top
End Sub

Private Sub cmdGo_Click()
    NavigateToPage (txtAddress.Text)
End Sub

Private Sub cmdHomePage_Click()
    NavigateToPage (HomePage)
End Sub

Private Sub cmdFinance_Click()
    NavigateToPage (FinancePage)
End Sub

Private Sub cmdTravel_Click()
    NavigateToPage (TravelPage)
End Sub

Private Sub cmdSearch_Click()
    WebBrowser1.GoSearch
End Sub

Private Sub cmdStop_Click()
  WebBrowser1.Stop
End Sub

```
Private Sub cmdRefresh_Click()
    WebBrowser1.Refresh
End Sub
Private Sub cmdBack_Click()
    'Add error handling for no previous history in the list
    WebBrowser1.GoBack
End Sub
Private Sub cmdForward_Click()
    'Add error handling for no more history in the list
    WebBrowser1.GoForward
End Sub
Private Sub cmdExit_Click()
    MsgBox "Remember to shut down the Internet software_
        and disconnect the phone!", 32, "Exit program"
    Unload WebForm
End Sub
Private Sub WebBrowser1_DocumentComplete(ByVal_
    pDisp As Object, URL As Variant)
    txtAddress.Text =_
        WebBrowser1.LocationURL
End Sub
```

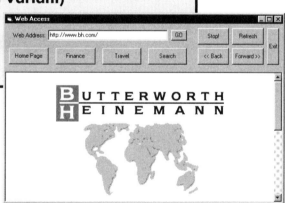

This chapter has provided a brief introduction to database and Internet application development. Visual Basic has many other options for external database access, allowing you to set up programs that will make use of databases on the user's computer, across a network or through the Internet. The theory behind the data-access and Internet processes is described in the on-line help, along with full details of controls, properties and methods. Although the operation of these processes can be complex, you can use them to create comprehensive and effective applications.

Exercises

1   Use Access to create a file of membership data, with the fields contained in the Member Details form from the Members program (Name, Address etc.)

2   Add a form to the Members program to allow you to import a record from the Access file; add a button to the main menu to load the import form.

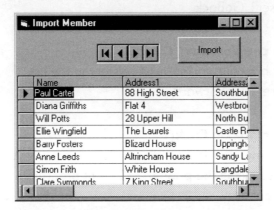

3   Add a form to the Members program to view a specific web site when a button is clicked on the Main Menu.

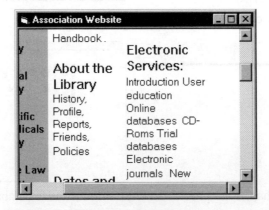

For solutions to these exercises, see page 193.

12 Solutions to exercises

1   Overview (p14)

1   Click on the Start button, Programs, the Microsoft Visual Basic 6.0 folder and the Microsoft Visual Basic 5.0 application icon. Double-click on Standard EXE.

The main window, toolbox, Project Explorer window, Properties window, Form Layout window and Form Designer window (containing Form1) should be visible (unless closed in a previous session).

2   Close windows by double-clicking on the Control-menu box or the Close button; re-open by selecting from the View menu or (for the Form Designer) double-clicking on Form1 on the Project Explorer window. Move windows by dragging the title bar; resize by dragging the edges or corners. Maximise by clicking on the Maximise button.

3   Click on the Help menu, then on Index. In the first box, type 'project e', double-click on 'Project Explorer' and select the 'Visual Basic Reference' topic from the list.

4   Click on the Minimise button in the main window.

Click on the Project1 button in the taskbar.

5   Click on File in the main window menu bar and then on Exit.

2   Forms (p26)

(Note that the dimensions of these forms do not have to be exactly as given below.)

1   In Windows Explorer, click on (C:) and then on File|New|Folder. Enter 'Members' as the name.

2   Change the properties for Form1 as follows:

Name:	frmMenu
Caption:	Member Manager
BorderStyle:	1 – Fixed Single
MinButton:	True
MaxButton:	False
Left, Top :	2145, 1230
Width x Height :	6735 x 6345

Save with File|Save Form1 As in the Members directory.

3   Use Project|Add Form to add a form. Change the properties as follows:

Name:	frmDetails
Caption:	Member Details
BorderStyle:	1 – Fixed Single
MinButton:	True
MaxButton:	False
Left, Top:	4050, 1155
Width x Height:	6750 x 5595

174

2   Forms (continued)

Save with File|Save Form1 As, naming it frmDetails.frm (or similar).

4   Use Project|Add Form to add a form. Change the properties as follows:

Name:	frmComments
Caption:	Comments
BorderStyle:	2 – Sizable (default)
MinButton:	True (default)
MaxButton:	True (default)
Left, Top:	1365, 3690
Width x Height:	6810 x 4005

Save with File|Save Form1 As, naming the file frmComments.frm (or similar).

5   Click on Project1 in the Project Explorer window, then change the Name in the Properties window to 'Members'.

6   Use File|Save Project As. When asked about SourceSafe, click on No.

7   Press **[F5]** to run the application. The first window should be displayed. Click on the Close box to close it down. Resave the project with File|Save Project.

3   Controls (p48)

1   Control properties are as follows:

Labels

Name:	lblTitle	lblMainMenu
Caption:	Member Manager	MAIN MENU
Alignment:	2 – Center	2 – Center
Font:	14 point, bold	12 point, bold
Left, Top:	720, 360	720, 960
Width x Height:	5175 x 375	5175 x 375

Command buttons

Name:	cmdMemberDetails	cmdComments
Caption:	&Member Details	&Comments
Default:	True	False (default)
Cancel:	False (default)	False (default)
Left, Top:	960, 4320	3720, 4320
Width x Height:	1815 x 495	1815 x 495

Name:	cmdExit
Caption:	E&xit
Default:	False (default)
Cancel:	True
Left, Top:	2640 x 5160
Width x Height:	1215 x 495

3 Controls (continued)

2 Use Project|Add Form to add a new form. Change the properties as follows:

Name:	frmPassword
Caption:	Password
BorderStyle:	3 – Fixed Dialog
ControlBox:	False
Left, Top:	2610, 2550
Width x Height:	4140 x 2805

Add the following controls:

Label

Name:	lblEnter
Caption:	Enter your &password:
Font:	10 point
Left, Top:	960, 360
Width x Height:	2055 x 255

Text box

Name:	txtPassword
Text:	(blank)
Font:	10 point
PasswordChar:	*
Left, Top:	960, 840
Width x Height:	2055 x 375

Command buttons

Name:	cmdOK	cmdCancel
Caption:	&OK	&Cancel
Default:	True	False
Cancel:	False	True
Left, Top:	480, 1560	2280, 1560
Width x Height:	1215 x 495	1215 x 495

Save the form as frmPassword.frm in the Members directory.

3 Control properties are as follows:

Frames

Name:	fraPersonal	fraMType
Caption:	Personal Details	Membership Type
Left, Top:	480, 1080	480, 3720
Width x Height:	5655 x 2295	1935 x 1215

Name:	fraSubs
Caption:	Subscription
Left, Top:	2640, 3720
Width x Height:	2295 x 1215

Label (form)

Name:	lblMemNo
Caption:	&Member No:
Alignment:	1 – Right Justify
Left, Top:	480, 300
Width x Height:	975 x 255

Text box (form)

Name:	txtMemNo
Text:	(blank)
Left, Top:	1560, 240
Width x Height:	1575 x 375

Labels (Personal Details)

Name:	lblName	lblAddress
Caption:	&Name:	&Address:
Alignment:	1 – Right Justify	1 – Right Justify
Left, Top:	240, 420	240, 1020
Width x Height:	1215 x 255	1215 x 255

Text boxes (Personal Details)

Name:	txtName	txtAddress
Text:	(blank)	(blank)
MultiLine:	False	True
Left, Top:	2040, 1440	2040, 2040
Width x Height:	3255 x 375	3255 x 1095

Option buttons (Membership Type)

Name:	optFull	optAssociate
Caption:	&Full	A&ssociate
Value:	True	False
Left, Top:	480, 360	480, 720
Width x Height:	1215 x 255	1215 x 255

Labels (Membership Type)

Name:	lblAmount	lblPaidOn
Caption:	Amoun&t:	&Paid on:
Alignment:	1 – Right Justify	1 – Right Justify
Left, Top:	240, 300	240, 780
Width x Height:	735 x 255	735 x 255

Text boxes (Membership Type)

Name:	txtAmount	txtPaidOn
Text:	(blank)	(blank)
Left, Top:	1080, 240	1080, 720
Width x Height:	975 x 375	975 x 375

3 Controls (continued)

Command buttons (form)

Name:	cmdOK	cmdCancel
Caption:	&OK	&Cancel
Default:	True	False
Cancel:	False	True
Left, Top:	5160, 3840	5160, 4440
Width x Height:	975 x 495	975 x 495

4 Control properties are as follows:

Text box

Name:	txtComments
Text:	(blank)
MultiLine:	True
ScrollBars:	2 – Vertical
Left, Top:	0, 0
Width x Height:	6690 x 2775

Command buttons

Name:	cmdOK	cmdCancel
Caption:	&OK	&Cancel
Default:	True	False
Cancel:	False	True
Left, Top:	1440, 3000	4035, 3000
Width x Height:	1215 x 495	1215 x 495

5 Save using File|Save Project. Run the program by pressing **[F5]**. You can click on any of the three Main Menu buttons but they will have no effect as yet.

Close the program with Run|End or by clicking on the Close button.

4 Coding events (p72)

(Note that, to save space, most blank lines have been removed from program listings.)

1 Display the frmMainMenu form, double-click on the Member Details button and enter the following procedure in the Code window:

```
Private Sub cmdMemberDetails_Click()
    frmDetails.Show
End Sub
```

2 Double-click on the Comments button and enter the following procedure:

```
Private Sub cmdComments_Click()
    frmComments.Show
End Sub
```

3 Double-click on the Exit button and enter the following procedure:

4 Coding events (continued)

```
Private Sub cmdExit_Click()
    Unload frmMainMenu
End Sub
```

Double-click on a blank area of the form. In the Procedure box, select Unload and enter the following procedure:

```
Private Sub Form_Unload(Cancel As Integer)
    Unload frmDetails
    Unload frmComments
End Sub
```

4   Double-click on a blank area of the form and enter the following procedure:

```
Private Sub Form_Load()
    frmMainMenu.Left = (Screen.Width – frmMainMenu.Width) / 2
    frmMainMenu.Top = (Screen.Height – frmMainMenu.Height) / 2
End Sub
```

5   Display the frmDetails form and add a combo box control with the following properties:

Label	
Name:	lblRegion
Caption:	Region:
Alignment:	1 – Right Justify
Left, Top:	3600, 300
Width x Height:	975 x 255

Combo box	
Name:	cboRegion
Text:	(blank)
Style:	0 – Dropdown Combo
Sorted:	True
Left, Top:	4680, 240
Width x Height:	1455 x 315

Double-click on a blank part of the form and add the following procedure:

```
Private Sub Form_Load()
    cboRegion.AddItem "North"
    cboRegion.AddItem "South"
    cboRegion.AddItem "East"
    cboRegion.AddItem "West"
End Sub
```

6   Double-click on the OK button and enter the following procedure:

```
Private Sub cmdOK_Click()
    Unload frmDetails
End Sub
```

4 Coding events (continued)

Double-click on the Cancel button and enter the following procedure:

Private Sub cmdCancel_Click()
```
    Unload frmDetails
End Sub
```

7   Display the Comments form and double-click on it. In the Procedure box in the top right of the window, select Resize and enter the following procedure:

Private Sub Form_Resize()
```
    txtComments.Height = frmComments.ScaleHeight – 825
    txtComments.Width = frmComments.ScaleWidth
    cmdOK.Top = frmComments.ScaleHeight – 600
    cmdCancel.Top = cmdOK.Top
    cmdOK.Left = frmComments.ScaleWidth / 2 – 690 – cmdOK.Width
    cmdCancel.Left = frmComments.ScaleWidth / 2 + 690
End Sub
```

(Later, you will need to add instructions to cope with the window being minimised or made too small to display the text box.)

8   Double-click on the OK button and enter the following procedure:

Private Sub cmdOK_Click()
```
    Unload frmComments
End Sub
```

Double-click on the Cancel button and enter the following procedure:

Private Sub cmdCancel_Click()
```
    Unload frmComments
End Sub
```

5 Variables (p94)

1   Set up the form and add the following procedures:

Private Sub cmdInchCm_Click()
```
    Dim Inches As Single, Cm As Single
    Const CmPerInch = 2.54
    Inches = Val(txtEntry.Text)
    Cm = (Int((Inches * CmPerInch * 100) + 0.5)) / 100
    txtResult.Text = Str(Cm)
    lblEntry.Caption = "Inches"
    lblResult.Caption = "cm"
End Sub
```

Private Sub cmdCmInch_Click()
```
    Dim Inches As Single, Cm As Single
    Const CmPerInch = 2.54
    Cm = Val(txtEntry.Text)
    Inches = (Int((Cm / CmPerInch * 100) + 0.5)) / 100
    txtResult.Text = Str(Inches)
```

5 Variables (continued)

```
        lblEntry.Caption = "cm"
        lblResult.Caption = "Inches"
    End Sub

    Private Sub cmdLbKg_Click()
        'Similar routine to cmdInchCm_Click with Const KgPerLb = 0.453
    End Sub

    Private Sub cmdKgLb_Click()
        'Similar routine to cmdCmInch_Click with Const KgPerLb = 0.453
    End Sub

    Private Sub cmdPintLitre_Click()
        'Similar routine to cmdInchCm_Click with Const LitresPerPint = 0.568
    End Sub

    Private Sub cmdLitrePint_Click()
        'Similar routine to cmdCmInch_Click with Const LitresPerPint = 0.568
    End Sub

    Private Sub txtEntry_Change()
        lblEntry.Caption = "(Entry)"
        lblResult.Caption = "(Result)"
        txtResult.Text = ""
    End Sub

    Private Sub cmdExit_Click()
        Unload frmUnits
    End Sub
```

The result box's enabled property should be False. None of the buttons has a Default property set to True.

2   If the combo box is left blank, ListIndex has a value of −1, so the Reps array must be redimensioned to allow for this. The procedure is as follows:

```
    Private Sub cboRegion_LostFocus()
        Dim Reps(-1 To 4) As String
        Dim SelectedRegion As Integer, Rep As String

        'Fill array (assume list box is sorted)
        Reps(-1) = "No selection"     'Box is blank
        Reps(0) = "M. Williams"       'East
        Reps(1) = "R. Walker"         'North
        Reps(2) = "J. Evans"          'South
        Reps(3) = "D. Clarke"         'West

        'Get selection number and display corresponding rep
        SelectedRegion = cboRegion.ListIndex
        Rep = Reps(SelectedRegion)
        lblRep.Caption = "Rep:   " & Rep
    End Sub
```

5 Variables (continued)

3   The following program uses two text boxes for entering the dates (txtDate1 and txtDate2) and two for showing the results (txtDays and txtWeeks). The calculation is initiated by clicking on a button (cmdCalculate).

```
Private Sub cmdCalculate_Click()
    Dim Days1 As Single, Days2 As Single
    Dim NumWeeks As Long
    Dim NumDays As Integer
    Days1 = DateValue(txtDate1.Text)    'Convert entries to date/time values
    Days2 = DateValue(txtDate2.Text)
    NumWeeks = Int((Days2 – Days1) / 7)   'Calculate weeks and days
    NumDays = (Days2 – Days1) Mod 7
    txtWeeks.Text = NumWeeks              'Display results
    txtDays.Text = NumDays
End Sub
```

6 Basic instructions (p120)

1   The procedure is as follows:

```
Public Sub AddDate(DateIn As Date, Period As String, _
        Extra As Integer, DateOut As Date, WDay As Integer)
    Dim Units As String
    Dim DayIn As Integer, MonthIn As Integer, YearIn As Integer
    Dim MonthOut As Integer, YearOut As Integer
    Units = UCase(Left(LTrim(Period), 1)) 'Get first character of Period
    DayIn = Day(DateIn)                'Extract date components
    MonthIn = Month(DateIn)
    YearIn = Year(DateIn)
    Select Case Units                  'Calculate new date
        Case "D"
            DateOut = DateIn + Extra
        Case "W"
            DateOut = DateIn + Extra * 7
        Case "M"
            MonthOut = MonthIn + Extra
            DateOut = DateSerial(YearIn, MonthOut, DayIn)
        Case "Y"
            YearOut = YearIn + Extra
            DateOut = DateSerial(YearOut, MonthIn, DayIn)
    End Select
    WDay = WeekDay(DateOut)            'Calculate weekday
End Sub
```

The following event procedure calls the calculation procedure:

```
Private Sub cmdCalculate_Click()
    Dim DateOut As Date, DateIn As Date
    Dim WeekOut As Integer
```

```
            DateIn = DateValue(txtDateIn.Text)
            AddDate DateIn, txtType.Text, Val(txtAdd.Text), DateOut, WeekOut
            txtResult.Text = DateOut
            txtDayNumber.Text = WeekOut
        End Sub
```

2   The function is as follows:

Public Function PasswordValid(Password As String) As Boolean

```
        'Add code here to read correct password from a file
        '(Assume correct password is "pass")
        If Password = "pass" Then
            PasswordValid = True
        Else
            PasswordValid = False
        End If
    End Function
```

3   The three controls at the top of the window have the following properties:

Combo box

Name:	cboMonth
Sorted:	False
Style:	2 – Dropdown list

Text box

Name:	txtYear
Text:	(blank)

Command button

Name:	cmdRedisplay
Caption:	Redisplay
Default:	True

The two control arrays have the following properties:

Text box

Name:	txtDiaryEntry
Text:	(blank)
Index:	0
Left, Top:	1440, 1080
Width x Height:	1215 x 375

Label

Name:	lblDayNo
Caption:	(blank)
Index:	0
Alignment:	1 – Right Justify
Left, Top:	1080, 1140
Width x Height:	255 x 375

Add the following procedures to the (General) section of the form:

Public Sub FillMonthBox()
```
    cboMonth.AddItem "January"
    cboMonth.AddItem "February"
    cboMonth.AddItem "March"
    cboMonth.AddItem "April"
    cboMonth.AddItem "May"
    cboMonth.AddItem "June"
    cboMonth.AddItem "July"
    cboMonth.AddItem "August"
    cboMonth.AddItem "September"
    cboMonth.AddItem "October"
    cboMonth.AddItem "November"
    cboMonth.AddItem "December"
End Sub
```

Public Sub LoadCalendar()
```
    Dim DCol As Integer, DRow As Integer, i As Integer
    txtDiaryEntry(0).Visible = False    'Hide original text box and label
    lblDayNo(0).Visible = False

    For DCol = 0 To 5                           'One column for each week
        For DRow = 0 To 6                       'One row for each day of the week
            i = (DCol * 7) + DRow + 1        'Calculate day number
            Load txtDiaryEntry(i)        'Load text box, display at correct offset
            txtDiaryEntry(i).Left = 1440 + 1560 * DCol
            txtDiaryEntry(i).Top = 1080 + 600 * DRow
            txtDiaryEntry(i).Visible = False
            Load lblDayNo(i)              'Load label, display at correct offset
            lblDayNo(i).Left = 1080 + 1560 * DCol
            lblDayNo(i).Top = 1140 + 600 * DRow
            lblDayNo(i).Visible = False
        Next DRow
    Next DCol
End Sub
```

Public Sub ViewCalendar(CalMonth As Integer, CalYear As Integer)
```
    Dim DCol As Integer, DRow As Integer, i As Integer
    Dim Started As Boolean, Finished As Boolean
    Dim FirstDay As Date, LastDay As Date
    Dim NumDays As Integer, DayNo As Integer

    FirstDay = DateSerial(CalYear, CalMonth, 1)        'Get first day of month
    LastDay = DateSerial(CalYear, CalMonth + 1, 1) – 1 'Calculate last day
    NumDays = Day(LastDay)              'Calculate number of days in month
    Started = False                    'Set initial values
    Finished = False
    DayNo = 1
```

```
            For DCol = 0 To 5            'One column for each week
                For DRow = 0 To 6            'One row for each day of the week
                    'For first column, check to see if this is first day of month
                    If DCol = 0 Then
                        If DRow + 2 = WeekDay(FirstDay) Or _
                                (DRow = 6 And WeekDay(FirstDay) = 1) Then
                            Started = True
                        End If
                    End If
                    i = (DCol * 7) + DRow + 1      'Calculate day number

                    'Display text box and label; increment day number
                    If Started And Not Finished Then
                        txtDiaryEntry(i).Visible = True
                        txtDiaryEntry(i).Text = ""
                        lblDayNo(i).Caption = DayNo
                        lblDayNo(i).Visible = True
                        DayNo = DayNo + 1
                    Else
                        txtDiaryEntry(i).Visible = False
                        lblDayNo(i).Visible = False
                    End If

                    If DayNo > NumDays Then   'Stop when last day
                        Finished = True          'has been displayed
                    End If
                Next DRow
            Next DCol
        End Sub
```

Add the following procedures to frmCalendar:

Private Sub Form_Load()
```
    Dim DefaultMonth As Integer, DefaultYear As Integer
    FillMonthBox                    'Fill combo box with month names
    LoadCalendar         'Add calendar boxes and labels but do not display

    'Set defaults as current year and month (index for January is 0)
    cboMonth.ListIndex = Month(Date) − 1
    txtYear.Text = Year(Date)

    'Display calendar for default year and month (December)
    DefaultMonth = cboMonth.ListIndex + 1
    DefaultYear = txtYear.Text
    ViewCalendar DefaultMonth, DefaultYear
End Sub
```

Private Sub cboMonth_Click()
```
    cmdRedisplay_Click
End Sub
```

6 Basic instructions (continued)

```
Private Sub txtYear_LostFocus()
    cmdRedisplay_Click
End Sub

Private Sub cmdRedisplay_Click()
    Dim CalendarYear As Integer, CalendarMonth As Integer
    CalendarYear = Val(txtYear.Text)    'Get year, month (ListIndex = 0 for Jan)
    CalendarMonth = cboMonth.ListIndex + 1
    ViewCalendar CalendarMonth, CalendarYear
End Sub
```

7 Error handling (p128)

1   Display the Member Details form and double-click on the Region combo box so that the Code window is displayed. Click on the first statement after the Dim lines in the cboRegion_LostFocus procedure and press **[F9]**.

Press **[F5]** to run the program, click on Member Details and select a Region. Click on any text box to break into the program.

Highlight lblRep.Caption and select Debug|Add Watch. Click on OK. Click on cboRegion in the code, select Debug|Add Watch and change the Expression to cboRegion.Text. Click on OK, then move the Debug window to a position where you can see it. Press **[F8]** to single-step through the program and watch the Debug window.

2   Amend the procedure as follows:

```
Private Sub cmdRedisplay_Click()
    Dim CalendarYear As Integer, CalendarMonth As Integer
    On Error GoTo BadYear
ErrorRestart:
    CalendarYear = Val(txtYear.Text)    'Get year, month (ListIndex = 0 for Jan)
    CalendarMonth = cboMonth.ListIndex + 1
    ViewCalendar CalendarMonth, CalendarYear
    Exit Sub
BadYear:
    MsgBox "Assuming this year", 32, "Year error"
    txtYear.Text = Year(Date)
    Resume ErrorRestart
End Sub
```

8 Menus (p136)

1   The menus and procedures are as follows:

```
Private Sub mnuFileExit_Click()
    cmdExit_Click
End Sub
```

```
Private Sub mnuWindowMemberDetails_Click()
    cmdMemberDetails_Click
End Sub
```

```
Private Sub mnuWindowComments_Click()
    cmdComments_Click
End Sub
```

```
Private Sub mnuWindowCloseAll_Click()
    Unload frmDetails
    Unload frmComments
End Sub
```

```
Private Sub mnuHelpAbout_Click()
    MsgBox "Member Manager v1.0", 64, "About Member Manager"
End Sub
```

2   The menus and procedures are as follows:

```
Private Sub mnuFileAbandon_Click()
    cmdCancel_Click
End Sub
```

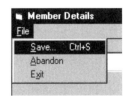

```
Private Sub mnuFileExit_Click()
    cmdOK_Click
End Sub
```

3   The menus and procedures are as follows:

```
Private Sub mnuFileAbandon_Click()
    cmdCancel_Click
End Sub
```

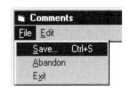

```
Private Sub mnuFileExit_Click()
    cmdOK_Click
End Sub
```

```
Private Sub mnuEditCut_Click()
    Clipboard.Clear
    Clipboard.SetText  txtComments.SelText
    txtComments.SelText = ""
End Sub
```

```
Private Sub mnuEditCopy_Click()
    Clipboard.Clear
    Clipboard.SetText  txtComments.SelText
End Sub
```

```
Private Sub mnuEditPaste_Click()
    txtComments.SelText = Clipboard.GetText()
End Sub
```

```
Private Sub mnuEditClear_Click()
    Dim DeleteAll As Integer
```

8   Menus (continued)

```
                    'MsgBox value 292 = Yes/No + Warning Query + 2nd button
                    DeleteAll = MsgBox("Delete all comments?", 292, "Delete comments")
                    If DeleteAll = 6 Then
                        txtComments.Text = ""          'Yes button pressed
                    End If
                End Sub
```

9   Files (p152)

1   Add the following controls:

Combo box
Name:	cboMemList
Style:	0 – Dropdown Combo
Text:	(blank)
Left, Top:	2040, 2040
Width x Height:	2415 x 315

Command button
Name:	cmdAddMember
Caption:	Add Member
Left, Top:	4680, 2040
Width x Height:	1215 x 315

Add the following procedure:

```
Private Sub cmdAddMember_Click()
    cboMembers.AddItem  cboMembers.Text
End Sub
```

2.   Use Project|Components to add the Microsoft Common Dialog Control to the toolbox. Add the following Common Dialog controls to the front-end form:

Name:	dlgOpen	dlgSave
Filter:	*.mem	*.mem
FileName:	*.mem	*.mem

Add the following line to (Declarations) in Members.bas:

```
Public Fname As String      'Member list filename
```

Add the following procedures to frmMainMenu:

```
Public Sub SaveMemberList()
    Dim i As Integer
    Open Fname For Output As #2      'Save data to file
    For i = 0 To cboMembers.ListCount – 1
        cboMembers.ListIndex = i
        Write #2, i + 1, cboMembers.Text
    Next i
```

```
        Close #2
    End Sub

    Private Sub mnuFileSaveAs_Click()
        dlgSaveAs.ShowSave              'Create new file
        Fname = dlgSaveAs.FileName
        If Right(Fname, 4) <> ".mem" Then
            Fname = Fname & ".mem"
        End If
        On Error GoTo FileError
        SaveMemberList                  'Save the member list
        Exit Sub
    FileError:
        MsgBox "Cannot save file " & Fname, 16, "Save File"
        Resume Next
    End Sub
```

3   Add the following procedures to frmMainMenu:

```
    Private Sub mnuFileSave_Click()
        On Error GoTo FileError
        SaveMemberList                  'Save the member list
        Exit Sub

    FileError:
        MsgBox "Cannot save file " & Fname, 16, "Save File"
        Resume Next
    End Sub

    Private Sub mnuFileOpen_Click()
        Dim RecNo As Integer
        Dim MemberName As String
        'Use standard dialog to get filename
        dlgOpen.Filter = "*.mem"             'Restrict to bmp files
        dlgOpen.FileName = "*.mem"           'Initial name to be displayed
        dlgOpen.ShowOpen                     'Display the box
        On Error GoTo FileError
        Fname = dlgOpen.FileName             'Fill the combo box
        Open Fname For Input As #1
        Do While Not EOF(1)
            Input #1, RecNo, MemberName
            cboMembers.AddItem  MemberName
        Loop
        Close #1
        Exit Sub

    FileError:
        MsgBox "Cannot open file " & Fname, 16, "Open File"
        Resume Next
    End Sub
```

4 Add the following procedures to frmComments:

```
Private Sub mnuFileSave_Click()
    Dim MemberName As String
    Dim CommentsFile As String
    On Error GoTo FileError
    'Construct filename
    MemberName = frmMainMenu.cboMembers.Text
    CommentsFile = MemberName & ".cmt"

    Open CommentsFile For Output As #3        'Write file
    Print #3, txtComments.Text
    Close #3
    Exit Sub
FileError:
    MsgBox "Cannot save file " & CommentsFile, 16, "Save Comments"
    Resume Next
End Sub

Private Sub cmdOK_Click()
    mnuFileSave_Click
    Unload frmComments
End Sub
```

5 Add the following procedures to frmComments:

```
Private Sub Form_Load()
    Dim MemberName As String
    Dim CommentsFile As String
    Dim FirstLine As Boolean

    CR = Chr(13) & Chr(10)              'CR/line feed
    On Error GoTo FileError
    MemberName = frmMainMenu.cboMembers.Text
    CommentsFile = MemberName & ".cmt"
    FirstLine = True                   'Read comments from file
    Open CommentsFile For Input As #3
    Do While Not EOF(3)
        Line Input #3, TextIn
        If FirstLine Then
            txtComments.Text = TextIn
            FirstLine = False
        Else
            txtComments.Text = txtComments.Text & CR & TextIn
        End If
    Loop
    Close #3

ExitProc:
    Exit Sub
```

9 Files (continued)

```
FileError:
    If Err <> 53 Then              'Ignore File Not Found error
        MsgBox "Cannot open file " & CommentsFile, 16, "Open Comments"
    End If
    Resume ExitProc
End Sub
```

6   Add the following procedures to frmDetails (Declarations):

```
Private Type DetailsType
    RecordNo As Integer
    MemberNo As String * 8
    Region As Integer
    Name As String * 40
    Address As String * 200
    MemType As Boolean
    Amount As Single
    PaidOn As Date
End Type
```

Add the following procedures:

```
Private Sub mnuFileSave_Click()
    Dim RecNo As Integer
    Dim DetailsFile As String
    Dim RecLen As Integer
    Dim DetailsRec As DetailsType            'Declare record variable

    On Error GoTo FileError
    'Construct filename and record number
    DetailsFile = Left(Fname, Len(Fname) – 4) & ".dtl"
    RecNo = frmMainMenu.cboMembers.ListIndex + 1
    DetailsRec.RecordNo = RecNo              'Build record
    DetailsRec.MemberNo = txtMemNo.Text
    DetailsRec.Region = cboRegion.ListIndex
    DetailsRec.Name = txtName.Text
    DetailsRec.Address = txtAddress.Text
    DetailsRec.MemType = optFull.Value
    DetailsRec.Amount = Val(txtAmount.Text)
    If Trim(txtPaidOn.Text) <> "" Then
        DetailsRec.PaidOn = DateValue(txtPaidOn.Text)
    Else
        DetailsRec.PaidOn = DateValue(Date)
    End If
    RecLen = Len(DetailsRec)                 'Write record
    Open DetailsFile For Random As #4 Len = RecLen
    Put #4, RecNo, DetailsRec
    Close #4
    Exit Sub
```

191

9   Files (continued)

```
FileError:
    MsgBox "Cannot save file " & DetailsFile, 16, "Save Details"
    Resume Next
End Sub
```

Private Sub cmdOK_Click()
```
    mnuFileSave_Click
    Unload frmDetails
End Sub
```

7.   Add the following procedures to frmDetails:

Private Sub Form_Load()
```
    Dim RecNo As Integer
    Dim DetailsFile As String
    Dim RecLen As Integer
    Dim DetailsRec As DetailsType     'Declare record variable
    On Error GoTo FileError
    cboRegion.AddItem "North"          'Fill Region box
    cboRegion.AddItem "South"
    cboRegion.AddItem "East"
    cboRegion.AddItem "West"
    If Len(Fname) < 4 Then        'Construct filename and record number
        Fname = "Dafault.mem"
    End If
    DetailsFile = Left(Fname, Len(Fname) – 4) & ".dtl"
    RecNo = frmMainMenu.cboMembers.ListIndex + 1
    RecLen = Len(DetailsRec)               'Read record
    Open DetailsFile For Random As #4 Len = RecLen
    If RecNo > 0 Then
        Get #4, RecNo, DetailsRec
    End If
    Close #4

    If DetailsRec.RecordNo <> RecNo Then 'Check for initial load of record
        DetailsRec.RecordNo = RecNo      'Record will contain rubbish so clear
        DetailsRec.MemberNo = ""
        DetailsRec.Region = 0
        DetailsRec.Name = ""
        DetailsRec.Address = ""
        DetailsRec.MemType = False
        DetailsRec.Amount = 0
        DetailsRec.PaidOn = Date
    End If

    txtMemNo.Text = Trim(DetailsRec.MemberNo)            'Build record
    If txtMemNo.Text = "" Then
        txtMemNo.Text = RecNo
    End If
```

9 Files (continued)

```
                    cboRegion.ListIndex = DetailsRec.Region
                    cboRegion_LostFocus

                    txtName.Text = Trim(DetailsRec.Name)
                    If txtName.Text = "" Then
                        txtName.Text = frmMainMenu.cboMembers.Text
                    End If
                    txtAddress.Text = Trim(DetailsRec.Address)

                    optFull.Value = DetailsRec.MemType
                    optAssociate.Value = Not DetailsRec.MemType

                    txtAmount.Text = Trim(DetailsRec.Amount)
                    txtPaidOn.Text = Trim(DetailsRec.PaidOn)

            ExitProc:
                Exit Sub

            FileError:
                If Err <> 53 Then          'Ignore File Not Found error
                    MsgBox Err & Error & "Cannot open " & DetailsFile, 16, "Open Details"
                End If
                Resume ExitProc
            End Sub
```

10 Graphics (p160)

1 Add an image control to frmMainMenu. Use its Picture property to select a bitmap. Set Stretch to True to make the bitmap fit the image area.

2 Add a Print option to the File menu and enter the following procedure:

```
Private Sub mnuFilePrint_Click()
    frmDetails.PrintForm
    frmComments.PrintForm
    'For a more sophisticated printout, combine the two forms into a new form
End Sub
```

11 External databases (p172)

1 Create the file with a Details table consisting of the field names shown on the Member Details form (excluding the Member Number). Split the address over a number of fields, one for each possible line. Save the file as Members.mdb.

2 Create a form named frmImport, with Caption 'Import Member'.

Use Project|Components to add the Microsoft ADO Data Control and Microsoft DataGrid Control to the toolbox.

Add an ADO Data control to the import form. Change the Name to datMembers.

Double-click on ConnectionString and click on Build. Select the Microsoft Jet Provider (choose the driver appropriate to your version of Access).

Click on Next. Select Members.mdb. Click on Test Connection. Close the dialogs.

Double-click on RecordSource. Set the Command Type to adCmdTable and the Table to Details. Click on OK.

Add a Data Grid control. Set the Name to grdMembers and the DataSource to datMembers. Right-click and select Retrieve Fields.

There is no need to change the fields that are displayed. Set the grid to a reasonable size within the form.

Add a command button with the name cmdImport.

Create the following procedure:

```
Private Sub cmdImport_Click()
    Dim CR As String
    Dim Region As String
    Dim MemDet As Variant
    CR = Chr(13) & Chr(10)

    'Retrieve data for selected row
    MemDet = datMembers.Recordset.GetRows(1)
    frmMainMenu.cboMembers.AddItem MemDet(0, 0)

    'Add member to list on main menu
    frmMainMenu.cboMembers.ListIndex =_
                    frmMainMenu.cboMembers.ListCount - 1

    'Copy details from selected row on grid to Details form
    frmDetails.Show

    'Fill Name box
    frmDetails.txtName.Text = MemDet(0, 0)

    'Combine individual address lines with CR/LF
    frmDetails.txtAddress.Text = MemDet(1, 0) & CR & MemDet(2, 0) & _
                    CR & MemDet(3, 0)

    'Set radio buttons according to value of text field
    If MemDet(4, 0) = "Full" Then
        frmDetails.optFull = True
    Else
        frmDetails.optAssociate = True
    End If

    'Fill Amount box
    frmDetails.txtAmount.Text = MemDet(5, 0)
```

```
'Fill Paid On box
frmDetails.txtPaidOn.Text = MemDet(6,0)

'Select position in combo box according to value of text field
Region = MemDet(7, 0)
Select Case Region
    Case "North"
        frmDetails.cboRegion.ListIndex = 1
    Case "South"
        frmDetails.cboRegion.ListIndex = 2
    Case "East"
        frmDetails.cboRegion.ListIndex = 0
    Case "West"
        frmDetails.cboRegion.ListIndex = 3
End Select
End Sub
```

Add a command button called cmdImportMember to frmMainMenu

Create the following procedure:

```
Private Sub cmdImportMember_Click()
    frmImport.Show
End Sub
```

Amend frmMainMenu's unload event procedure as follows:

```
Private Sub Form_Unload(Cancel As Integer)
    Unload frmDetails
    Unload frmComments
    Unload frmImport
End Sub
```

3   Create a form named frmWebsite with the Caption 'Association Website'.

Use Project|Components to add the Microsoft Internet Controls to the toolbox.

Add a Web Browser component to the form.

Add the following procedure:

```
Private Sub Form_Resize()
    WebBrowser1.Top = 0
    WebBrowser1.Left = 0
    WebBrowser1.Height = frmWebsite.ScaleHeight
    WebBrowser1.Width = frmWebsite.ScaleWidth
End Sub
```

Add a command button named cmdWebsite to frmMainMenu.

Create the following procedure:

```
Private Sub cmdWebsite_Click()
    frmWebsite.Show
    frmWebsite.WebBrowser1.Navigate ("<Put URL here>")
End Sub
```

You now have a basic application which can be extended to suit specific applications.

Index